Soulful
Affirmations

May each affirmation be a blessing!

Soulful Affirmations

365 DAYS OF POSITIVE THOUGHTS AND LESSONS TO START YOUR DAY

CHERYL POLOTE-WILLIAMSON

publish
your gift

SOULFUL AFFIRMATIONS

Copyright © 2021 Cheryl Polote-Williamson

All rights reserved.

Published by Publish Your Gift®
An imprint of Purposely Created Publishing Group, LLC

Printed in the United States of America

ISBN: 978-1-64484-365-9 (print)
ISBN: 978-1-64484-366-6 (ebook)

Special discounts are available on bulk quantity purchases by book clubs, associations and special interest groups. For details email: sales@publishyourgift.com or call (888) 949-6228.

For information log on to www.PublishYourGift.com

Acknowledgments

First, I would like to thank God the giver of life and the one from whom all blessings flow. With God's grace, mercy, and favor nothing is impossible. I also would like to thank my husband, Russell Williamson Sr.; my children: Russell Jr., Lauren, and Courtney; my grandbabies: Leah and Russell III; and family members and friends for supporting me throughout my journey.

I especially want to thank the "Affirmations with Cheryl" Facebook Group. Because of your decision to affirm yourself and my witnessing the manifestations that occurred in your life, this book was birthed. I truly thank you from the bottom of my heart!

Also, I would like to acknowledge and thank all of the frontline and essential workers that put their lives on the line to serve others daily. I want you to know that you are affirmed, valued, and loved by God! May the love of God continue to protect and cover you!

Peace, love, and blessings to all!

Foreword

~~~~~~

I was blessed to meet Cheryl Polote-Williamson last year in Atlanta when I attended my first meeting of Film Fatales (an advocacy group for female directors). It was at the private home of one of the members and I didn't know anyone, except for the friend who encouraged me to become a member. This friend also brought Cheryl along with her, since Cheryl was visiting from Dallas and had come to town to get more information on the film industry, as she was writing and producing her first movie script.

After the meeting was over, I walked out to my car, along with Cheryl and our girlfriend, and this is where the true purpose for us connecting unfolded. For some reason, Cheryl started asking me where I wanted to go with my career. She also asked about my family. I literally broke down. I was shocked at myself because I felt like nothing was wrong. I love my career, I love my family, and I love my life. But suddenly I realized that I'd been carrying a lot, yet still holding it together like so many women do. By speaking with Cheryl that night and really receiving the blessings of her words and prayers, a friendship, mentorship, and purposeful relationship was sparked.

You see, though I LOVE my life and I've experienced great successes both personally and career wise, I've constantly felt as though I was in a state of proving myself and my value—to others, but also to myself. Cheryl saw all of that in me during a 15-minute conversation standing outside of my car. She immediately stepped right into her purpose of healing by reminding me of my worthiness and greatness. This is who Cheryl is and what she does. She shared herself with me, as she does with the world. Affirming through affirmations is her superpower!

There's not a day that goes by that I do not speak power and love into myself by speaking affirmations. The one that I boldly say and write down in a journal EVERY DAY is "I believe in me!" It took me a while to say it and longer to feel it, but through my friend Cheryl, my daily meditation and affirmations, and my faith in God, I know I'm equipped with all I need to succeed at whatever God has put on my mind and in my heart to do. I am worthy and I don't have to prove that to anyone. I am the gift, just like you are. Strengthen your mind and spirit by saying the daily affirmations in *Soulful Affirmations*. See how the words pour into your greatness EVERY DAY!

With love,
Terri J. Vaughn
Actress, Director, Producer

Introduction

Understanding the power of words has totally shaped my life. Whether by example or experience, from childhood to now, I have been privy to the transformative energy and influence of the words from our mouth and the meditation of our heart. I watched my parents have what they say for years. I also watched them give, give, give, expecting nothing from anyone but God. For me, putting a vision, goal, or desire in sight, considering it done and confirming the acceptance of it with positive and affirming words, then giving and doing for others like I already had what I asked for was learned behavior. I'm glad to have digested such a life altering principle early because many did not.

It has become my mission and my joy to teach others the authority of affirmations. I have seen businesses, families, and lives transform before my very eyes through positive words, thoughts, and actions. The belief that affirmations work is something off which I cannot be moved. As long as I continue to see the fruit and benefit of affirmations in my life and the lives of those around me, I will push affirming words as a vital part of the journey to obtaining the life you want.

We must get in a conscious habit of thinking higher than our circumstances allow. We must push the obstacles we see before us aside and dare to speak life to our desires, goals, surroundings, and ourselves. You are more than you think you are. You are greater than your issues have indicated. You are loved. You are magic. You deserve more! It is time to adopt these truths once and for all. You have to know you're a winner even if no one else does, and you must say so every day of your existence. I have purposed to be an example of the truth that creating this habit works. It has worked for me and for others time and time again. I know it will work for you.

To help you on your passage to finding out the best about and thinking the most of yourself, it is with great joy that I present *Soulful Affirmations*, the latest addition to the Soul Series. *Soulful Affirmations* brings the affirming words and soul-stirring lessons of 68 co-authors into one place for a daily guide of prayer, meditation, confessions of faith, and mindset challenges. Grow in the areas of faith, love, peace, joy, kindness, and self-awareness (including: assuredness, self-esteem, strength, power, and confidence). Develop in business, finances, and more; but, most of all, grow and develop in God's mindfulness and love for you and be changed forever.

Soulful Affirmations is 365 days of thoughts, words, and actions that will change the way you see yourself and life. It is my prayer that you join me, and the thousands of others who have discovered the power of affirmations, and allow these impactful and awakening lessons to flush out the negativity and excuses and pour into you new life, positivity, and all the reasons you deserve to win.

JANUARY 1

~~~~~~

I am being transformed by the renewing of my mind.

—Cheryl Polote-Williamson

Romans 12:2

"And be not conformed to this world: but be ye transformed
by the renewing of your mind, that ye may prove what
is that good, and acceptable, and perfect, will of God."

You aren't just here. You have a purpose. And if you are
already walking in your purpose, God has greater.
If you can still see your vision and purpose plainly, or what
you're doing doesn't feel bigger than you, then
God definitely has more in store. To get on His page for
your life, you must renew your mind daily with affirming
words, positive thoughts, and actions. Only then will you
begin proving that there truly is no limit to what He
has for you and what you can achieve.

Soulful Affirmations

JANUARY 2

~~~~~~

I am what I say.

—Traci Henderson Smith

John 1:14

"And the Word was made flesh, and dwelt
among us, and we beheld his glory."

What came first is what God said. He took what He said
and wrapped it in flesh: Christ—The Living Word. This
Living Word was in Him; it was Him. It was life and
light—the spoken expression of God's inner self. What
we say is the spoken expression of our inner self. It is
the interpretation of our thoughts. Words offer people an
explanation of what we think of ourselves. You are the
embodiment of what you say. What you say is alive and tells
others what you think of yourself. Speak well of yourself
and allow the glory within you to shine.

JANUARY 3

~~~~~~

I keep my mind focused on achieving my goals.

—Tammy L. Woodard

Proverbs 16:3 (NIV)

"Commit to the LORD whatever you do,
and he will establish your plans."

Oftentimes, we allow distractions and procrastination to keep us from accomplishing our goals. It is the enemy's job to get you off task by bombarding your mind with thoughts that stifle you. You must make a decision to not allow people, places, and things to get you off track. Stay focused!

JANUARY 4

~~~~~~

I replace my fears with faith.

—Minister Kiesha L. Peterson

2 Timothy 1:7

"For God hath not given us the spirit of fear; but of power, and of love, and of a sound mind."

Seasons of fear can serve many purposes, such as: showing us we need to strengthen our faith, confirming how much our faith in God has grown, or simply allowing us to stand on His Word. So, believe and confess that no matter what fear breeds, the power of love and a sound mind will always overcome that spirit.

JANUARY 5

~~~~~~

I will take action to walk in my success.

—Danette M. Brown

Jeremiah 29:11 (NIV)

"'For I know the plans I have for you,' declares
the LORD, 'plans to prosper you and not to harm you,
plans to give you hope and a future.'"

We all create great blueprints to start a project, a business,
go back to school, or just succeed in life, but many of us
never activate the plans to see the outcome. As a believer,
God has plans for your life to flourish beyond your wildest
dreams. What is holding you back from walking into your
future and trusting Him?

JANUARY 6

I am excited to motivate others.

—Sandra Reese Jolla

1 Thessalonians 5:11

"Wherefore comfort yourselves together, and edify
one another, even as also ye do."

I am my brother's keeper. As I am strengthened, I will also
lift and strengthen others. I get excited when I can bring joy,
happiness, and motivation to others' lives and situations. An
attitude of joy helps me through life's challenging moments.
Just as the caterpillar struggles to make it out of its tight
cocoon, we can be the agents who help others spread
their wings and soar like bright and brilliant butterflies!

JANUARY 7

~~~~~~

I speak truth, life, and blessings over my future.

—Dr. Peggie Etheredge Johnson

1 Peter 3:10 (NLT)

"If you want to enjoy life and see many
happy days, keep your tongue from speaking
evil and your lips from telling lies."

In what ways are your words repelling the life you desire
because they are maligned and malicious? The words
that emerge from our mouth are often returned upon our
own lives. Refrain your lips from speaking negativities,
fabrications, and obscurities. Speak words that convey
longevity, truth, and bountiful blessings to certify that your
days are plentiful, peaceful, and prosperous.

Soulful Affirmations

JANUARY 8

~~~~~~

I am prosperous in every area of my life.

—Juanita Payne

3 John 1:2

"Beloved, I wish above all things that thou mayest prosper and be in health, even as thy soul prospereth."

Do you know that being prosperous is more than having a lot of money? Do you know that excellence is our God-given right? You have the power to create a life of choice and wellness, both physically and spiritually. Through God, we have the authority to declare and decree life over our well-being.

JANUARY 9

~~~~~~

I walk, talk, and live in power.

—Frances Ann Bailey

Ephesians 3:20 (NIV)

"Now to him who is able to do immeasurably
more than all we ask or imagine, according
to his power that is at work within us."

No more pity parties. Work your power. Do you know that according to this Scripture, you have the ability to speak and even think things according to the will of God, then watch things shift and manifest? Stop adapting to things that you want to change. You are an environment shifter, a mind shifter, and a powerful force to be reckoned with. It is time for you to walk in the power God has given you.

JANUARY 10

~~~~~~

I am listening and trusting in God's direction for my life.

—Lynder E. Scott, MBA

Isaiah 50:10 (NIV)

"Who among you fears the LORD and obeys the word of his servant? Let him who walks in the dark, who has no light, trust in the name of the LORD and rely on his God."

There may have been times that you sought outside council. Their advice sounded good to the ear, but not to your soul. That was God's nudge to you saying, "Hey, what about asking me?" Seek His advice first. It may not sound comfortable to your ears; however, your soul will be peaceful.

JANUARY 11

~~~~~~

I pursue perfection and arrive at excellence.

—Dr. Madge L. Barnes

Psalm 139:14 (NIV)

"I praise you because I am fearfully and wonderfully made; your works are wonderful, I know that full well."

We all want to be the best at our endeavors. But did you know that our spiritual DNA provides the building blocks to accomplish our goals, dreams, and aspirations? Our thoughts can hinder or help us to be the best. As it is said in the sports arena: "You are the G.O.A.T. (Greatest of All Time).

JANUARY 12

I expect and receive increase, abundance, and overflow every day.

—Anissa Green Dotson

Mark 11:24 (NIV)

"Therefore I tell you, whatever you ask for in prayer,
believe that you have received it, and it will be yours."

What are you asking God for? Do you believe or ask amiss?
I remember meditating on a position, even while pumping
gas. As I prayed, I thanked God. Eventually, the phone call
came. God wants us to bring Him into remembrance
of His Word and believe we have it!

JANUARY 13

~~~~~~

I have the courage to create.

—Lashunda Denby

Proverbs 23:7 (NASB)

"For as he thinks within himself, so he is."

A requirement for developing your vision is imagination.
The special ingredients for having the courage to create
are: a dream and boldness. Think outside the box;
do not put limitations on yourself or others while in
pursuit of your dreams. Constantly push yourself to
expand and learn. Do not compromise your creativity
because someone doesn't support it.

JANUARY 14

I am surrounded by favor.

—LaToya Adams

Psalm 5:12 (NKJV)

"For You, O Lord, will bless the righteous; With favor You will surround him as with a shield."

The favor of God is a defense; it covers and protects those who are righteous. His favor equates to safety, prosperity, protection, and opportunity. Its value is kingdom currency, and when applied to our daily living there is literally nothing on Earth that can hinder its efficacy in our lives.

JANUARY 15

~~~~~~

I declare that I am blessed and blessings are chasing me down.

—Tiffany Mayfield

Deuteronomy 28:2 (NIV)

"All these blessings will come on you and accompany you if you obey the Lord your God."

Your words carry enormous power to heal, destroy, encourage, break, to tell your truth or deceive, and to praise or to criticize. The power of your words can be the key to your success or the reason for your downfall. God can bless your life through the words you speak. What words are you speaking over your life?

Soulful Affirmations

JANUARY 16

~~~~~~

I will be intentional about using my gifts and skillset to serve.
—Natasha M. Harris

1 Peter 4:10 (NIV)

"Each of you should use whatever gift you have
received to serve others, as faithful stewards
of God's grace in its various forms."

If you frequently wonder what you can do to serve
others, oftentimes, it is right in front of you. Think about
one of your gifts. Now think about how it can help your
community. Next, by getting involved and using your gifts,
you are giving God the glory.

JANUARY 17

~~~~~~

*I walk in clarity, prosperity, and purpose. God
has ordered my steps and He directs me.*

—Alesha Brown, The Joy Guru

Psalm 32:8

"I will instruct thee and teach thee in the way which
thou shalt go: I will guide thee with mine eye."

How many times have you tried something new or taken
a leap of faith? Often, there is great fear and anxiety
preceding your act of boldness. From this point forward, go
in boldness and power knowing that God is guiding your
steps and has gone before you. Favor is yours!

JANUARY 18

~~~~~~

I think positive thoughts that produce positive
results in my life and in the lives of others.

—Contessah Irene Davis

Philippians 4:8 (NASB)

"Finally, brethren, whatever is true, whatever is honorable, whatever is right, whatever is pure, whatever is lovely, whatever is of good repute, if there is any excellence and if anything worthy of praise, dwell on these things."

Whatever controls your mind also controls your destiny because it controls your actions. Therefore, make it a daily practice to take captive every negative thought and change it to a positive thought that will eventually produce positive outcomes.

JANUARY 19

~~~~~~

If I can see it, I can have it.

—Vivian Grafton

Joel 2:28 (NIV)

"And afterward, I will pour out my Spirit on all people.
Your sons and daughters will prophesy, your old men
will dream dreams, your young men will see visions."

Have you ever seen someone doing something that you
could see yourself doing? According to the prophet Joel,
sons and daughters shall prophesy what they see and
hear, old men shall have dreams, and young men shall see
visions. What have you seen or dreamed lately? Go do it!

Soulful Affirmations

JANUARY 20

〜〜〜〜〜〜〜〜〜〜〜〜〜〜〜〜〜〜〜〜〜〜〜〜〜〜〜〜

I give myself permission to exhale negativity and inhale positivity.
—Marsha Taylor

Proverbs 17:22 (NIV)

"A cheerful heart is good medicine, but a
crushed spirit dries up the bones."

As I walked down the lonely community trail early
one morning before the break of day, 1 was bombarded
with a bevy of conflicting thoughts. It felt like I woke
up on the wrong side of the bed. As I questioned myself,
I knew this was wrong!

My spirit man was reminded that whenever I make the
Lord the joy of my thoughts, He becomes my strength.
Reclaim your cheerful heart today!

JANUARY 21

~~~~~~

I am not weak nor defeated; I am strong!

—Renee Denise Fowler

2 Corinthians 12:10 (TPT)

"I'm not defeated by my weakness, but delighted!
For when I feel my weakness and endure
mistreatment—when I'm surrounded with troubles
on every side and face persecution because of my
love for Christ—I am made yet stronger. For my
weakness becomes a portal to God's power."

In society, weakness is often seen as a sign of defeat. But
if in your weakness, you learn to trust and depend on God,
you will find that weakness is the portal that gives you
access to God's power!

Soulful Affirmations

JANUARY 22

~~~~~~

Money flows to me freely.

—Roni Benjamin

Deuteronomy 28:12 (NWT)

"Jehovah will open up to you his good storehouse, the heavens, to give your land rain in its season and to bless all that you do. You will lend to many nations, while you yourself will not need to borrow."

The Law of Attraction is the ability to attract into our lives whatever we are focusing on. Are you focusing on the turmoil of your current situation? Instead, focus on the daily activities that will result in the life you want—a life flowing with peace and prosperity.

JANUARY 23

~~~~~~

I am equipped to make this day great.

—Ruby Jeanine Batiste

Psalm 145:2 (NIV)

"Every day I will praise you and extol
your name for ever and ever."

We all experience days when we dread getting
out of bed because our minds are full of overwhelming
thoughts. But, when we praise and bless God
through every moment of our day, He will equip us to
thrive in uncertainty and adversity. What actions
will you take today to praise the Lord?

Soulful Affirmations

JANUARY 24

I will courageously do all things with love.

—Russell M. Williamson

1 John 4:18 (NIV)

"There is no fear in love. But perfect love drives out fear."

It's very likely that we will have a moment in
which we are hesitant and even stopped by our
fears—fear of rejection, fear of the unknown, or
fear of failure just to start. Recognizing that we are children
of God and that He protects us because He loves us
perfectly and completely, we should move with purpose
and humble confidence. Step into the day with faith,
knowing that you are loved by the Almighty.

JANUARY 25

~~~~~~

I am born to win.

—Dr. Madeline J. Anderson Thomas

1 John 5:4 (ESV)

"For everyone who has been born of God
overcomes the world. And this is the victory
that has overcome the world—our faith."

Belief governs behavior. No one is a failure until they accept
and believe that they are a failure. You are a winner when
you accept and believe by faith that you are a winner. God
placed in you everything that you need to be a winner.

JANUARY 26

~~~~~~

I am unbreakable; my confidence in God is soaring.

—Marie Hart

Hebrews 13:6 (NIV)

"So we say with confidence, 'The Lord is my helper; I will not be afraid. What can mere mortals do to me?'"

We may think that we can manage on our own, but the fact is that our confidence grows out of our dependence on God. We will have victory when we place our confidence in God, not ourselves.

JANUARY 27

~~~~~~

My body is a fat burning machine.
—Shawntelle Y. Jones

1 Corinthians 9:26 (NLT)
"So I run with purpose in every step.
I am not just shadowboxing."

What do you do to keep your body healthy? Do you eat a
well-balanced meal? Do you exercise several times a week?
Do you visit your physician regularly? God has given us one
body and one life to live. Make it count.

JANUARY 28

~~~~~~

I accept, activate, and assert my authority to fulfill my divine callings.
—Michelle Winfield Fuqua

Genesis 1:28 (WEB)

"Be fruitful, multiply, fill the earth, and subdue it. Have dominion... over every living thing that moves on the earth."

God sees you exactly as He created you. No person or situation can negate your purpose. He has given you access to the resources for your assignment. You are called, equipped, and empowered to complete every dream in your heart. What is standing in your way?

JANUARY 29

~~~~~~

I JUMP because I know the parachute will open.

—Necole Martinez

Deuteronomy 31:6 (NIV)

"Be strong and courageous. Do not be afraid or terrified
because of them, for the LORD your God goes with
you: he will never leave you nor forsake you."

Have you ever not done something because of fear?
Have you stayed in a deadbeat relationship, job, or
friendship because of fear? Fear can be debilitating
and will stunt your growth. When we are led by God,
we walk in faith. Faith tells you that without a shadow of a
doubt, things will work out!

Too many times, we stopped believing because we
stopped proceeding! Do it anyway and know that
things will work out according to God's plan!

Soulful Affirmations

JANUARY 30

~~~~~~

I will not let fear of success stop me.

—Nina Gaddie Howard

Philippians 4:6 (NIV)

"Do not be anxious about anything, but in every situation, by prayer and petition, with thanksgiving, present your requests to God."

Doubt can be a crippling emotion. You can become frozen and transfixed on all of the reasons things will not work. Instead of standing still, pray and move while trusting God! Go after your dreams in faith and peace, knowing you will succeed.

JANUARY 31

~~~~~~

I will follow the instruction manual (the Bible).

—Sonya M. Hall-Brown

Isaiah 48:17 (NKJV)

"Thus says the LORD, your Redeemer, The Holy One
of Israel: 'I am the LORD your God, Who teaches you
to profit, Who leads you by the way you should go.'"

"Will a man rob me (God)... in tithes and offerings?" If you
want different results in your finances, you have to do some
things differently. When it's time to pay your bills, lay them
in your sacred place, and begin to shout and give God the
highest praise because it is He who supplies all our needs.
Are you willing to be obedient by planting your seed and
waiting for the harvest?

Soulful Affirmations

FEBRUARY 1

I choose to attract love, peace, and happiness.

—Marie Hart

Galatians 5:22-23

"The fruit of the Spirit is love, joy, peace, longsuffering, gentleness, goodness, faith, meekness, temperance."

You have to love yourself first before you can love anyone else. We often grapple with putting ourselves first but it is never wrong to love yourself. You have to love every part of yourself in order to attract love, peace, and happiness.

FEBRUARY 2

I am loved, cherished, and significant for I have found GRACE from God Almighty!

—Alesha Brown, The Joy Guru

Genesis 6:8

"But Noah found grace in the eyes of the Lord."

Don't you let this world tell you that there is so much more you must accomplish to be significant. God regretted that He made man and was ready to destroy EVERYONE. But ONE MAN found grace in the eyes of God and was spared. Beloved, you are that ONE!

FEBRUARY 3

~~~~~~

I am seen and known to the Creator. He sees me and He loves me.
—Melissa Powell-Harrell

Genesis 16:13 (NIV)

"She gave this name to the LORD who spoke to
her: 'You are the God who sees me,' for she said,
'I have now seen the One who sees me.'"

El Rai is the God Who Sees Me. I am not invisible to Him.
He loves me. He listens to my humble cry and answers at
the sound of my voice. He inclines His ear to hear from me.
I am, I can, I shall, and I will be all that He declared.

FEBRUARY 4

~~~~~~

I will be careful who I give my heart to because I deserve the best.

—L. Lorraine Hale-Cooper

Jeremiah 29:13

"And ye shall seek me, and find me, when ye
shall search for me with all your heart."

It is good to be loved by the right person. It is also
good to know when to walk away because your heart has
not been treasured and respected as it should have been.
God knows what's best; search for Him. He is waiting
and knows how to handle your heart. Are you letting
the right person love you?

FEBRUARY 5

~~~~~~

I will prove myself only to myself.

—Cynthia Fox Everett

James 1:25 (NKJV)

"But he who looks into the perfect law of liberty and continues in it, and is not a forgetful hearer but a doer of the work, this one will be blessed in what he does."

As humans, we want to prove who we are to others, to belong or for approval. You can't change your past, you can only accept your present and turn the pages to a better future. The only person you need to prove anything to is yourself.

FEBRUARY 6

~~~~~~

I am a virtuous woman. My husband has full confidence in me.

—Tanya M. Turner

Proverbs 31:10-11 (NIV)

"A wife of noble character who can find? She is worth far more than rubies. Her husband has full confidence in her."

Positive statements regarding marriage are great for single and married women. Affirming what you believe, and extending happiness and gratitude is an act of faith. Repeating affirmations daily encourages us to be confident and to become better versions of ourselves. You are what you believe! What are you believing for in your marriage?

Soulful Affirmations

FEBRUARY 7

~~~~~~

I am fortunate to have people who love and value me.

—Danielle McGruder

John 15:12

"This is my commandment, That ye love
one another, as I have loved you."

God gave us the blueprint, His commandment, on
how He wants us to love and value others. We should do
everything with love, just as He loved us. Agape love is
pure, expecting nothing in return. How will you spread love
to others in the way our Father has done unto us?

FEBRUARY 8

I deserve genuine love despite my past mistakes.

—Cynthia Fox Everett

Ephesians 1:7 (NKJV)

"In Him we have redemption through his blood, the forgiveness of sins, according to the riches of His grace."

When you think of love, are you haunted by a less than perfect past? When Jesus was born and died on the cross for us, we were redeemed and created in His likeness and image. Love is who you are, not who you used to be.

FEBRUARY 9

~~~~~~

My heart belongs to the Lord.

—Danette M. Brown

Matthew 6:24

"No man can serve two masters: for either he will hate the one, and love the other; or else he will hold to the one, and despise the other. Ye cannot serve God and mammon."

Do you know when you put anything (people, cars, clothes, a house, or money) before God, you are serving two masters? To understand God's love for us, we must change our mindset and how we view ourselves. Having God at the head of our lives is all we need. Who do you serve?

FEBRUARY 10

~~~~~~

I refuse to compromise my relationship with God.

—Janie Lacy

1 Corinthians 13:13 (NIV)

"And now these three remain: faith, hope and love.
But the greatest of these is love."

Do not preoccupy yourself with people who God did not
ordain to be in your life! If you want the kind of energy that
will attract your soulmate, it starts with knowing your value
and loving yourself. God honors the sanctity of marriage.
To fulfill God's love on this journey, you must uphold
biblical principles and interdependence.

FEBRUARY 11

~~~~~~

I generously share my love and compassion for others.

—Yumica Thompson

1 John 4:7 (NKJV)

"Beloved, let us love one another, for love is of God; and everyone who loves is born of God and knows God."

Oftentimes, when we have been hurt, it is not easy to show others our love for them out of fear of rejection and pain. However, God is love and He instructs us to love one another so that we can love others the way that He loves us. For hurt is but a moment; love is for a lifetime.

FEBRUARY 12

~~~~~~

I choose to look in a full-length mirror, daily.

—Yvette #theEXCHANGE McGill

Psalm 139:14 (NIV)

"I praise you because I am fearfully and wonderfully
made; your works are wonderful, I know that full well."

I had allowed other people to make me believe that all I
had was a cute face and long hair. It took me losing my hair
to truly appreciate the fact that GOD makes no mistakes. I
now TRULY believe that I am perfectly made in HIS image.

Soulful Affirmations

FEBRUARY 13

I am single, satisfied, and waiting.

—Shaundre Emmerson

1 Corinthians 13:4 (NIV)

"Love is patient, love is kind."

Have you ever dreamed your fairy tale would end? Happily married, separated, then divorced. Struggling and blaming yourself. You are finally free. Take back your power and build yourself up: therapy, workshops, and fellowships will do. A treasure and a queen you are. Remember to love yourself and know your worth. Be patient with an open heart. What God has for you is for you.

FEBRUARY 14

I choose to love on purpose.

—Juanita Payne

1 Thessalonians 3:12 (NIV)

"May the Lord make your love increase and overflow for each other and for everyone else, just as ours does for you."

Do you know that when we choose to love on purpose, it's unconditional with no set limitations? When we choose to love completely and unconditionally, fear is removed. It covers, it forgives. "God commendeth his love toward us, in that, while we were yet sinners, Christ died for us."

Soulful Affirmations

FEBRUARY 15

~~~~~~

*I am a helpmate and God is preparing
the man He created just for me.*

—Tammy L. Woodard

Genesis 2:21 (NIV)

"So the LORD God caused the man to fall into a deep
sleep; and while he was sleeping, he took one of the
man's ribs and then closed up the place with flesh."

Why am I still single? Why can't I find the
right man? The answer is simple. God wants the best
for us and He knows the desires of our heart. Like Adam,
God is performing a surgical procedure on that perfect
mate. He's shaping and molding him or her to create
something wonderful! God wants you to trust Him, be
patient, and worship while you wait!

FEBRUARY 16

~~~~~~

I trust God and keep my focus on Him.
—Dr. Madeline J. Anderson Thomas

Proverbs 37:4 (NIV)

"Take delight in the Lord, and he will give
you the desires of your heart."

Trust God and focus your attention on Him and He will give
you the desires of your heart. God will provide the desires
of your heart when you make Him the singular joy of your
heart, the object of your faith, and the source of your hope.

FEBRUARY 17

I am in love with today because I have made peace with yesterday.

—Necole Martinez

2 Corinthians 5:17 (NIV)

"Therefore, if anyone is in Christ, the new creation has come: The old has gone, the new is here!"

So many times, we are ashamed of our past mistakes, experiences, hiccups, and path. Where we've come from and what we've done have all been designed to lead us down a path of greatness. We wear masks to cover up, hide, and bury those slip-ups, but we must honor those experiences. Once we honor them, we can make peace with them. Inner peace is the ultimate joy of love!

FEBRUARY 18

I seek balance and make my family a priority.

—Natasha M. Harris

Psalm 133:1 (NIV)

"How good and pleasant it is when God's people live together in unity!"

Family is a beautiful thing! Despite how busy life may be, along with living in different states or countries, family should be a priority. Take time to show your appreciation. From phone calls, to sending notes in the mail, to virtual family fellowship time remember that family unity, togetherness, and legacy should remain a priority.

Soulful Affirmations

FEBRUARY 19

I will no longer carry dead weights in relationships.
—Dr. Madge L. Barnes

Hebrews 12:1 (NIV)

"... let us throw off everything that hinders and the sin that so easily entangles. And let us run with perseverance the race marked out for us..."

It is often easy to become involved in a situation that drains and drags you down. Those closest to you can drain you the most if you don't take a stance. One day, you decide that enough is enough and God honors your stance. You are too valuable to settle for futile disagreements with people who will never agree with you. Save your time and energy for the matters that matter.

FEBRUARY 20

I will nurture the greatness within me.

—Nina Gaddie Howard

John 15:16 (NIV)

"You did not choose me, but I chose you and appointed you so that you might go and bear fruit."

God has created you for greatness. In order to grow and bear much fruit, you need to be confident in your faith, selective in your nourishment, and consistent in your self-care. I challenge you to sprinkle seeds of love along your journey.

FEBRUARY 21

~~~~~~

My life, family, and relationships are whole.

—Traci Henderson Smith

John 10:10 (NKJV)

"The thief does not come except to steal, and to kill, and to destroy. I have come that they may have life, and that they may have it more abundantly."

You are the gatekeeper of your life and relationships. Your plan is peace, prosperity, and being of good use and service to others. Recognize what disrupts the plan by robbing you of your peace, stealing and killing relationships and opportunities, and sifting life. Set up safeguards to protect what's rightfully yours. More importantly, don't be your own enemy.

FEBRUARY 22

~~~~~~

*I am at peace knowing that God's goodness, love,
and mercy follow me throughout my day.*

—Ruby Jeanine Batiste

Psalm 23:6 (NIV)

"Surely your goodness and love will follow
me all the days of my life, and I will dwell
in the house of the LORD forever."

God promised His goodness and mercy will be with us all
the days of our lives. Reflect on how you have witnessed
God's faithful love throughout your life. It is amazing how
His goodness, mercy, and love chases us down! He will
never leave us. We are His for eternity.

FEBRUARY 23

I will guard my heart.

—Juanita Payne

Proverbs 4:23 (NIV)

"Above all else, guard your heart, for everything you do flows from it."

We control what we allow in and out of our hearts, which determines our actions. God does not want us to guard our heart by ourselves. He wants us to guard our heart with His Word. Guarding our heart allows us to guard our thoughts, beliefs, and attitude.

FEBRUARY 24

*I am a beacon of light and positive influence
to all within the sound of my voice.*

—Cynthia Drummond Andrews, MBA

Matthew 5:16 (NIV)

"In the same way, let your light shine before
others, that they may see your good deeds
and glorify your Father in heaven."

No matter what you may be experiencing this day, be
reminded that God has a purpose for you and your life. God
equipped you for today before this challenge presented
itself. Step into your purpose knowing that God ordered
your steps and He has already worked things out for you.

Soulful Affirmations

FEBRUARY 25

~~~~~~

I never sow seeds of discord among friends or foes.

—Contessah Irene Davis

Proverbs 17:9 (NASB)

"He who conceals a transgression seeks love, But he
who repeats a matter separates intimate friends."

Don't be so quick to expose people when they
have done you wrong. It is one of the things that God
hates the most. Use wisdom in how you handle
information regarding others and avoid gossiping so
that you are not an agent of division.

FEBRUARY 26

~~~~~~

I use discernment in all of my relationships.

—Charlene E. Day

Hosea 14:9 (NLT)

"Let those who are wise understand these things. Let those
with discernment listen carefully. The paths of the Lord
are true and right, and righteous people live by walking
in them. But in those paths sinners stumble and fall."

Relationships are important. It's critical who you connect
with. Manage expectations. Don't ignore signs of toxicity.
Like Eve, you've been given dominion over your garden.
Your choices impact everyone. Who have you allowed into
your garden? Toxicity can be avoided by honoring your
beliefs and values and listening to discernment.

Soulful Affirmations

FEBRUARY 27

~~~~~~

I will not construct my own fortress, God is my fortress.

—Fatima Williams

Psalm 18:2

"The LORD is my rock, and my fortress, and my deliverer;
my God, my strength, in whom I will trust; my buckler,
and the horn of my salvation, and my high tower."

Have you ever emotionally built a wall to protect
yourself from life's disappointments or heartbreaks?
When a person is faced with repeated hurts, sometimes
they will attempt to form an emotional wall to block
the pain. God is our fortress; He is our high tower!
God forms a covering that is constantly around us.
Will you trust God to shield and protect you?

FEBRUARY 28

~~~~~~

I will stop following my heart.

—Anitra Green

Jeremiah 17:9

"The heart is deceitful above all things, and
desperately wicked: who can know it?"

The world would have you believe that following
your heart is best, but a believer knows to follow the
Bible and the voice of the Lord. The Word of the Lord is
consistent and true. It is never changing, never deceitful,
the opposite of wicked, and it will never lead you astray.
Make a declaration today to STOP following your heart
and follow the Word of the Lord instead.

Soulful Affirmations

MARCH 1

~~~~~~

It's my time.

—Dr. Eric L. Holmes

Psalm 102:13

"Thou shalt arise, and have mercy upon Zion: for
the time to favour her, yea, the set time, is come."

There has been a shifting in the earth and the world,
but we are in the time of God's favor. Hold on, and in just
a little while things are going to fall into place. It's our time
and favor is upon us. We waited and we held on, now
the release is here. Don't compromise what you
waited so long for; it was worth the wait.

MARCH 2

~~~~~~

My dreams will come true.

—Heidi Lewis

Jeremiah 29:11 (LEB)

"For I know the plans I'm planning concerning
you,' declares Yahweh, 'plans for prosperity and not
for harm, to give to you a future and a hope.'"

Life isn't a random series of events. All of your experiences
have been predetermined by God. Yes, the hard places, the
times you've been misunderstood, and when you thought
you couldn't handle the pressures of life. God knew you
could handle it. He wants you to know He's always had you
in mind. He has the very best just for you. Close your eyes.
Can you visualize it? Go after your dreams!

Soulful Affirmations

MARCH 3

I am courageous.

—Dr. Sonya Wade Johnson

1 Corinthians 16:13 (NIV)

"Be on your guard; stand firm in the
faith; be courageous; be strong."

It is common for someone to say, "Stay strong and keep
the faith" or "Stand firm on what you believe." Sometimes,
saying those things is easier than actually doing them.
God has given us the strength we need to be courageous in
all situations. He has never lost a battle and He never will.
Keep showing up and so will God!

MARCH 4

I am God's workmanship in Christ.

—Bishop Richard S. Johnson

Ephesians 2:10 (NKJV)

"For we are His workmanship, created in Christ
Jesus for good works, which God prepared
beforehand that we should walk in them."

Are you walking in the power and authority of who
God created you to be? Have you allowed Christ to prepare
you for greatness? You belong to the Creator. That means
that He is responsible for you and all that pertains to you.
God designed a plan for your life before you were born.
Valiantly submitting to His design allows you to
participate in all of His glory created for you.

Soulful Affirmations

MARCH 5

~~~~~~

I am confident that I will finish all that God has assigned me to do.

—Michelle Franklin

Philippians 1:6

"Being confident of this very thing, that he
which hath begun a good work in you will
perform it until the day of Jesus Christ."

Has it ever felt like life was trying to stop you from
completing what you knew God told you to do? Has
sickness played a part in delaying you from reaching your
destiny? You don't have to worry anymore. If He started a
work in you, He will finish it. Just submit to His process!

MARCH 6

~~~~~~

I will change my language.

—Myoshi Robinson Thomas

Proverbs 18:20 (NIV)

"From the fruit of their mouth a person's stomach is filled; with the harvest of their lips they are satisfied."

I had to learn to speak better in order to be happy and successful. When you speak well, it can bring prosperity and success to all parts of your life. I learned that a good trait of speaking correctly is making sure my words are gracious and wise. What can possibly hinder you from using this simple rule for advancement?

Soulful Affirmations

MARCH 7

~~~~~~

I am stronger than I think.

—Royleta Foster

Isaiah 41:10 (MSG)

"Don't panic. I'm with you. There's no need to fear
for I'm your God. I'll give you strength. I'll help you.
I'll hold you steady, keep a firm grip on you."

Oftentimes, when met with challenges, we think we cannot
handle them but God tells us different. God tells us that He
will be the strength we need. When was the last time you
allowed God to be your strength?

MARCH 8

~~~~~~

I bring hope to those lost in despair.
For my frontline workers.

—Sherry Wurgler

Lamentations 3:21-23 (ESV)

"But this I call to mind, and therefore I have hope:
The steadfast love of the LORD never ceases,
his mercies never come to an end; they are new
every morning; great is your faithfulness."

You bring hope to those desperately in need during
this time of crisis. You are valuable and trustworthy. You
bring a calm, soothing word and touch to those in suffering.
You are a calm and confident presence in all of my
interactions. You connect and communicate well with peers
for the well-being of your patients. You are capable and
confident to give the best care to patients. You live
and breathe servant leadership skills to your peers.
You are collaborative and compassionate with co-workers.
You go the extra mile. You are enough!

MARCH 9

~~~~~~

I am completely healthy.

—Shameka Oliver

Isaiah 53:4-6 (NRSV)

"But he was wounded for our transgressions, crushed for our iniquities; upon him was the punishment that made us whole, and by his bruises we are healed."

The good news: The sacrifice of the Savior makes healing possible for all who call on Him.

MARCH 10

~~~~~~

I am secure in God's plans for my life.

—Dr. Sheila Bunton

Proverbs 3:5 (NIV)

"Trust in the Lord with all your heart."

Do you trust God's plans for your life like you trust in man-made inventions? How many times have you locked your car door or enabled your house alarm without giving a second thought or worry that once set you were secure? This is the same level of trust God requires from us to believe in His promises. What will you do differently to be secure in God's promises? What things do you need to trust God with today?

MARCH 11

I am not my circumstance. I AM victorious!

—Shameka D. Johnson

1 Corinthians 15:57 (ESV)

"But thanks be to God, who gives us the victory through our Lord Jesus Christ."

There will always be a circumstance to overcome or even memories from the past that haunt us as we move into our future. It can be daunting. It can be scary. However, take peace in the fact that your past does NOT define you! Through God, we have the victory and we truly reign supreme should we CHOOSE to. Choose YOU! What are you letting go of today?

MARCH 12

~~~~~~

I attract money. Call me "The money magnet."

—Lashunda Denby

Deuteronomy 8:18 (NIV)

"But remember the Lord your God, for it is he who gives you the ability to produce wealth, and so confirms his covenant, which he swore to your ancestors, as it is today."

There is always plenty of capital for those who can create practical plans for using it. Make yourself indispensable and efficient in what you are now doing, then you will attract the favorable attention of those who have the power to promote you into more responsible work that is to your liking.

MARCH 13

~~~~~~

I live according to my authentic purpose and original design.

—Traci Henderson Smith

Ephesians 2:10

"For we are his workmanship, created in Christ
Jesus unto good works, which God hath before
ordained that we should walk in them."

There is an original us, then there is the us we become
after tragedy, trauma, or someone's destructive words,
thoughts, or actions. It's often hard to get back to who we
were before the pain—the us God designed and called. We
spend so much time entangled with who we've become.
We build lives, families, businesses, and ministries around
who we've become rather than how we were made. Push
back against life's circumstances. Stand stronger, yes, but
declare unapologetically an authentic life filled with God's
original purpose and design.

MARCH 14

~~~~~~

I am a giver, and I will give to someone in need today.

—Deborah A. Smith

Proverbs 3:9 (NLT)

"Honor the LORD with your wealth and with
the best part of everything you produce."

Giving blesses the receiver and the giver. Today, think
about all the many ways you can give to someone in
need. You can give of your time, a listening ear, advice, or
monetary gifts. No matter how you give, remember the
LORD sees it and He will reward you in due season.

MARCH 15

I live with renewed strength.

—Denise Polote-Kelly

Isaiah 40:31 (NIV)

"but those who hope in the LORD
will renew their strength."

Have you ever felt so tired and beat down that all you could do was sit in a quiet place and hope for the strength to keep going? How many times have you experienced failure and setbacks? We are going to experience some trials, let downs, and disappointments but God will be God if we trust Him. When you are still and quiet, that's when God renews your spirit and fills you with His supernatural power. When we trust God, we open ourselves up to all He has to offer us. Only He can provide you with the power of renewal, but you must choose to accept His promise with your whole heart, mind, and spirit.

MARCH 16

~~~~~~

God has infused me with greatness beyond my comprehension.

—Joyce Brown, 2019 Ms. Texas Senior America

Ephesian 3:20 (NKJV)

"Now to Him who is able to do exceedingly abundantly above all that we ask or think."

God wants to do amazing things in your life. His plan for your life is bigger than you can imagine. God wants to blow your mind! To receive extraordinary blessings, you must have faith that God can and will transform you beyond what you think is possible. Achieving these extraordinary goals will be uncomfortable and will require you to stretch yourself. What unimaginable dreams and goals will you pursue?

MARCH 17

~~~~~~

I embrace the risks needed for changes to come to fruition.

—Alicia L. Hemphill

Isaiah 30:19 (BSB)

"He will surely be gracious when you cry for
help; when He hears, He will answer you."

Do your big dreams remain unfulfilled? You are wired to
achieve greatness. The reward of the dream is proportional
to the risk you must take to see the promise come to pass.
You should not avoid making a difficult decision. What
major challenge are you willing to embrace today?

MARCH 18

~~~~~~

I am determined to believe God.

—Angela Thomas

Matthew 19:26 (NIV)

"Jesus looked at them and said, 'With man this is impossible, but with God all things are possible.'"

Have you ever looked back and wondered how you got through what seemed to be a never-ending life situation? God in His Sovereignty is all-powerful and has supreme authority over EVERYTHING. As children of God, when we cry out "Abba," He has got to show up on the scene. No matter what your "it" is, trust that God can and will come through.

MARCH 19

I am blessed to be a blessing to someone every day.

—Anissa Green Dotson

Deuteronomy 28:3 (NIV)

"You will be blessed in the city and blessed in the country."

Sometimes, you may find yourself discouraged.
The baby keeps crying, the kids need money for school,
and you are pulled in numerous directions. Feeling
overwhelmed? Let go and give it to God. His grace is
sufficient. Go find someone in need and bless them,
then watch how God blesses you.

MARCH 20

~~~~~~

I make healthy choices with my money.

—Chartonna "CeCe" Woodley

Malachi 3:10 (NLT)

"'Bring all the tithes into the storehouse so there will be enough food in my Temple. If you do,' says the Lord of Heaven's Armies, 'I will open the windows of Heaven for you. I will pour out a blessing so great you won't have enough room to take it in! Try it! Put me to the test!'"

Do you believe God wants to give you an increase and overflow? Do you believe when God makes you a lender, you will not look for anything in return? Do you believe that God blesses the person that He knows will do the right thing? He will.

I am a leader who inspires action.

—Tangie Barkley Robinson

1 Peter 5:3 (ESV)

"not domineering over those in your charge,
but being examples to the flock."

What kind of leader are you? We are all leaders whether we want to be or not. We lead in our marriages, in our relationships, at our jobs, with our children, and at church. How do you want to influence the people around you? I challenge you to be the example you want to see.

MARCH 22

~~~~~~

I am walking in victory.

—Tara Johnson

1 Corinthians 15:57 (NIV)

"But thanks be to God! He gives us the
victory through our Lord Jesus Christ."

Whatever battle you are facing, God has already given you
the victory. Nothing is too hard for God. Even when you
cannot see the other side, know that He has already gone
before you. Trust that He knows what is best and wants
you to be victorious. So, stay the course, do the work, and
keep the faith. I challenge you to claim your blessing and
proclaim that victory is yours.

Soulful Affirmations

MARCH 23

~~~~~~

I will achieve my hopes and dreams.

—Taylor Spells

2 Chronicles 15:7 (NIV)

"But as for you, be strong and do not give
up, for your work will be rewarded."

Achieving your dreams is no easy task, but God is
accompanying you. Do you want to give up and throw
in the towel? Well, God will hand that towel right back to
you and give you the strength that you need to succeed.
Working towards goals can be a difficult task, but you
have to keep going. God won't let you quit on your
dreams and neither should you.

MARCH 24

~~~~~~

*I am intentional about EVERYTHING I set my
hands to do despite distractions.*

—Alesha Brown, The Joy Guru

Nehemiah 6:3b

"I am doing a great work, so that I cannot
come down: why should the work cease,
whilst I leave it, and come down to you?"

Just because you set your hands to do a great work
does not mean you are exempt from lies, distractions,
hindrances, or naysayers. As a matter of fact, you should
expect them. It is vital that you do all things with the proper
intent and clarity. Nothing great is exempt from challenges.

MARCH 25

~~~~~~

I will free myself from blocks.

—Charlene E. Day

John 8:36 (NIV)

"So if the Son sets you free, you will be free indeed."

The reason most of us don't pursue our goals is because of the blocked experiences that hinder our movement. These blocks are known as distractions. Ask yourself, "Is this issue more important than the goal I've set? Can it wait?"

When you identify what the block is you will free yourself.

MARCH 26

I praise God with a loud voice.

—Melissa Shiver Sumpter

Luke 17:15 (NIV)

"One of them, when he saw he was healed,
came back, praising God in a loud voice."

Has the Lord healed your body or delivered you from
something? Have you ever gone back to tell Him thank you?
There were so many times during our lives that if the Lord
didn't intervene, we wouldn't be here. So, in a loud
voice, tell the Lord thank you!

Soulful Affirmations

MARCH 27

I am the righteous daughter of the King and the heir to His riches.
—Tammy L. Woodard

Philippians 4:19 (NIV)
"And my God will meet all your needs according
to the riches of his glory in Christ Jesus."

You are a child of the King. God has riches stored
up waiting for you. Develop a relationship with Him.
He is your provider and He wants you to have what you
decree. Start thanking Him in advance for what you want.
Gratitude builds the multitude.

MARCH 28

~~~~~~

God's faithful promises are my armor and protection.

−Dr. Angela Kinnel

Psalm 91:4 (NLT)

"He will cover you with his feathers. He
will shelter you with his wings. His faithful
promises are your armor and protection."

There are 8,810 promises in the Bible. Of those
promises, 7,487 were made by God. We know that God
cannot lie. If He said it, it is so! All we are charged to do is
believe and trust Him at His word. God is faithful!
His promises never expire.

MARCH 29

~~~~~~

I am surrendering all to God; this is my reality for life.

−Lynder E. Scott, MBA

1 Peter 5:6 (NIV)

"Humble yourselves, therefore, under God's mighty hand, that he may lift you up in due time."

Contemplation infiltrates the mind. Does this happen to you? #Metoo. Reason being, we have left the door to our heart ajar for the enemy to set that bait of procrastination. Now that we know this, let's P.U.S.H (Pray Until Situations are Heard).

After this action, trust that God will work things out for your good because you have been selected to receive His favor.

MARCH 30

~~~~~~

I am a change agent.

—Sandra Reese Jolla

Philippians 4:13 (NKJV)

"I can do all things through Christ who strengthens me."

Have you ever created something from scratch?
I constantly embrace the adage: "The sky's the limit,"
by *Don Quixote,* because it reminds me that I can achieve
whatever I set my mind, heart, and soul to do. Believing
this assures me that my creative ideas and achievements
are reachable because I am not operating on my finite skills
but partnering with God who is infinite in His. Because
He strengthens me, I can make a difference. I put
Him first in all of my endeavors.

Soulful Affirmations

MARCH 31

~~~~~~

I am exactly where God intends for me to be in this moment.
—Cynthia Drummond Andrews, MBA

Proverbs 3:6

"In all thy ways acknowledge him, and
he shall direct thy paths."

Many times, we may have regretted choices we have
or have not made. Be mindful that God does not make
mistakes and where you are today is exactly where
He has intended for you to be. Know that the experiences
and the exposure you have had are all leading you to
and preparing you for your destiny. Thank God for His
divine guidance and interventions.

APRIL 1

I trust God to be the protector of my soul.

—Alicia L. Hemphill

Genesis 12:3 (NIV)

"I will bless those who bless you, and
whoever curses you I will curse."

Have you been accused of being hard to get to know?
Survivors of abuse can desire relationships but fear letting
others who are willing to help them achieve their destiny
get close. Kingdom life expands when we engage others
with intimacy and transparency. Are you willing to trust
God to protect your heart?

Soulful Affirmations

APRIL 2

*I don't fear my enemies. My ways please
God and peace surrounds me.*

—Alesha Brown, The Joy Guru

Proverbs 16:7

"When a man's ways please the LORD, he maketh
even his enemies to be at peace with him."

Many times, we fear what we perceive others think
about us and the ways they might try to sabotage us,
our efforts, and our success. But the Lord is able to
make even your enemies serve you and bless you if
the situation demands it. Go in peace.

APRIL 3

~~~~~~

*I am submitting to God's commands, resisting
the devil, and winning every battle.*

—Dr. Peggie Etheredge Johnson

James 4:7 (NKJV)

"Therefore submit to God. Resist the
devil and he will flee from you."

Are you in the thick of a spiritual battle with the enemy of
your soul and resisting his schemes as he flees?
We are forewarned to watch and pray in every battle; our
adversary is not flesh and blood. When we explicitly follow
the instructions of our spiritual commander-in-chief,
we win every battle. Our arsenal of spiritual weapons
will cause the enemy to flee when we submit to God's
choice of strategies and artilleries.

APRIL 4

~~~~~~

I embrace God's purpose for my life.

—Ruby Jeanine Batiste

Romans 8:28 (NIV)

"And we know that in all things God works
for the good of those who love him, who have
been called according to his purpose."

God's purpose for our lives isn't laid out in a straight,
smooth path. Our journey to purpose will take us through
several experiences; some will be pleasant and others will
not. What steps will you take today to embrace the ups and
the downs on your road to purpose filled living?

APRIL 5

*I am a warrior prepared to overcome every
challenge that presents itself.*

—Russell M. Williamson

James 1:3 (TPT)

"For you know that when your faith is tested it
stirs up power within you to endure all things."

There are days when we get overwhelmed by our
circumstances; however, God asks us to have faith in Him.
If we humble ourselves to Him, He will be our strength
in every moment of weakness. God has placed
everything within you that is required to handle
every situation that you will confront.

Soulful Affirmations

APRIL 6

~~~~~~

Everything I touch prospers.

—Traci Henderson Smith

Psalm 1:3 (AKJV)

"And he shall be like a tree planted by the rivers of water, that brings forth his fruit in his season; his leaf also shall not wither; and whatever he does shall prosper."

Did you know that you were built to prosper? From the beginning of creation, your instructions were to be fruitful (bring forth) and multiply (expand). No afterthought. No contingency plan. Just do it. Deuteronomy 8:18 even says, "God has given us the power to gain wealth," just don't forget Him when you get it. As believers, we must draw on the power within us to bring forth, expand, and prosper.

APRIL 7

I will be the beacon of strength to those who are weary.
For my frontline health care heroes.

—Sherry Wurgler

Matthew 11:28 (NIV)

"Come to me, all of you who are weary and
burdened, and I will give you rest."

You greeted a patient in recovery with a smile
and a spoonful of ice chips
I saw that
You sat and listened to a lonely patient whose
family could not visit
I saw that
You comforted a grieving mother with the news
that her child had just died
I saw that
You smiled into your patient's eyes and held his
hand as he took his last breath
Tears spilled like a waterfall from your eyes
I saw that
I see you
Thank you!

Soulful Affirmations

APRIL 8

~~~~~~

I will not be anxious today.

—Dr. Madeline J. Anderson Thomas

Philippians 4:6 (NIV)

"Do not be anxious about anything, but in every situation, by prayer and petition, with thanksgiving, present your requests to God."

Everyone gets anxiety occasionally. Different circumstances can cause anxiety. However, when faced with anxiety, God's directions are simple. God guides us to present our request in prayer with thanksgiving. Today, make "anxious for nothing" your goal. Will you replace anxiety with prayer today?

APRIL 9

~~~~~~

I will speak positive words over my life.

—Royleta Foster

Proverbs 18:20 (NCV)

"People will be rewarded for what they say;
they will be rewarded by how they speak."

What are you speaking over your life? Are you
speaking negative or positive things? Positive things bring
positive rewards from God. I know that life can sometimes
have its tests, but always remember that God only wants
what is good for your life. Speak positive things over your
life and those connected to you. What positive things
have you spoken over your life?

APRIL 10

~~~~~~

I deserve abundance.

—Roni Benjamin

Philippians 4:19 (NWT)

"In turn my God will fully supply all your need according to his riches in glory by means of Christ Jesus."

Born and raised in poverty, it's no wonder I felt hopeless like a penny with a hole in it. It's easy to succumb to self-limiting beliefs. Instead, choose to listen to the inner voice that softly whispers, "You have greatness within you." Live full and die empty knowing that you fulfilled your dreams and goals.

APRIL 11

~~~~~~

I walk on the path that leads to a beautiful life!

—Renee Denise Fowler

Psalm 16:11 (VOICE)

"Direct me on the path that leads to a beautiful life.
As I walk with You, the pleasures are
never-ending, and I know true joy and contentment."

We are often led off of the beautiful path by the allure of
worldly desires. How often have you sought to achieve a
goal, but became distracted? As we walk with God, He
promises to direct us to a beautiful life. What can you do
today that will place you on the path to your beautiful life?

Soulful Affirmations

APRIL 12

~~~~~~

I am a vessel full of Holy Ghost power.

—Myoshi Robinson Thomas

Acts 1:8 (NIV)

"But you will receive power when the Holy Spirit comes on you; and you will be my witnesses in Jerusalem, and in all Judea and Samaria, and to the ends of the earth."

Once we realize that we have Holy Ghost power, we become unstoppable. The things we used to be fearful of, we now face with a plan. Knowing that we hold the power to just speak to a thing and it be resolved is absolutely amazing. Knowledge is power.

APRIL 13

~~~~~~

I am who God says I am.

—Min. Kiesha L. Peterson

Romans 8:1 (ESV)

"There is therefore now no condemnation
for those who are in Christ Jesus."

Why do we believe the words of those who did not create
us? Why is it so hard to believe the words of our Creator?
How often do you look in the mirror and wonder who you
are? Society reminds you of who you are not. Remember
that we are created in God's image. We are His perfect
creation. Stop listening to the words of society. Start
listening to the voice of your Creator—God!

Soulful Affirmations

APRIL 14

~~~~~~

I step into my assured victory and make bold moves daily.

—Michelle Winfield Fuqua

Romans 8:37 (WEB)

"No, in all these things, we are more than conquerors through him who loved us."

You are victorious, even on the days that you have felt like the biggest loser. God loves you, supports you, and works on your behalf. Do not let failure diminish your faith. Get right back up and do it again until you get the result that God showed you.

APRIL 15

I command my mind to stay liberated since God has set me free.

—Michelle Franklin

Philippians 2:12

"Wherefore, my beloved, as ye have always obeyed, not as in my presence only, but now much more in my absence, work out your own salvation with fear and trembling."

Oftentimes, we're taught to focus on edification from others. But I am reminded that the greatest edification comes when we learn to empower ourselves. God gives us strength and power to empower ourselves before releasing us to empower others. Allow Him to take the lead. He'll walk you into freedom.

Soulful Affirmations

APRIL 16

I set my mind on the goodness of God.

—Sonya M. Hall-Brown

Philippians 4:8 (ESV)

"Finally, brothers, whatever is true, whatever is honorable, whatever is just, whatever is pure, whatever is lovely, whatever is commendable, if there is any excellence, if there is anything worthy of praise, think about these things."

How you think affects every area of your life. If you allow negative thoughts to fill your mind, you become a negative person. If you fill your mind with positive thoughts, you become a positive person. This promise invites you to focus your mind on the good and positive things in life.

APRIL 17

~~~~~~

I will trust the process!

—Denise Polote-Kelly

Matthew 6:25 (NIV)

"Therefore I tell you, do not worry about your life, what you will eat or drink; or about your body, what you will wear. Is not life more than food, and the body more than clothes?"

Worry is a choice. Do not worry about everyday life! Life consists of more than food, clothing, and things. Life is about living longer and worrying less. Anxiety is short-lived if we give it to God. Will you choose to worry, or will you choose to trust God? Worry changes nothing!

Soulful Affirmations

APRIL 18

I will let my pain push me forward to my destiny!
—Melissa Powell-Harrell

Philippians 4:13 (NIV)
"I can do all this through him who gives me strength."

Things happened in our lives that we must push past. We must push past fear, rejection, pain, abuse, disappointment, depression, and our past itself. The world needs us. We must push past the doubt to the dream. Push forward, and do not allow pain to push you backward.

APRIL 19

~~~~~~

Abundance is my portion and I accept nothing less.

—Dr. Sheila Bunton

John 10:10(b) (CSB)

"... I have come so that they may have
life and have it in abundance."

Have you ever wondered what it really means to walk in
abundance? Abundance means so much more than just
material stability. Abundance means to walk in the fullness
of God's strength and His joy in every area of our being—
spirit, body, and soul. Because it is God's will for us to
prosper in our entire being, in what areas do you need to
speak the abundance and fullness of God into your life?

Soulful Affirmations

APRIL 20

~~~~~~

My heart guides my speech.

—LaToya Adams

Luke 6:45 (NKJV)

"A good man out of the good treasure of his
heart brings forth good . . . For out of the
abundance of the heart his mouth speaks."

There is much to be said of a person's character by their
speech. Good people fill the treasure chest in their hearts
with goodness and faith. People who speak words of
affirmation will usually lead a holistic life of prosperity. The
power to guide your tongue and command your every move
is only possible by conducting a daily heart check.

APRIL 21

~~~~~~

I am a beacon of light for those in need of
inner healing and restoration.

—Tanya M. Turner

Matthew 5:16 (NIV)

"In the same way, let your light shine before
others, that they may see your good deeds
and glorify your Father in heaven."

To God be the glory in all that we do! As we evoke
inner healing, self-awareness, and restoration after trauma,
we gain the ability to evolve into our higher, authentic
selves. Then, we are able to live in the moment, utilize
our gifts, and be a light for others.

APRIL 22

~~~~~~

I embrace the "destiny warrior" within me.

—Marsha Taylor

Hebrew 10:36 (ESV)

"For you have need of endurance, so that when you have done the will of God you may receive what is promised."

Did I just hear you say, "I don't have what it takes."

Have you ever been told that?

It doesn't take much to derail our thoughts and peace of mind when we encounter days like those. Sometimes a comment from a neighbor, co-worker, or friend may cause you to self-sabotage into pity, hopelessness, or helplessness.

Remember there is a warrior inside of you.

You are stronger than you think and more resilient than you know!

APRIL 23

~~~~~~

I will cry to God as needed and continue on my path of success.

—L. Lorraine Hale-Cooper

Psalm 27:7

"Hear, O LORD, when I cry with my voice: have
mercy also upon me, and answer me."

Sometimes, you may call someone to cry out to them,
but they are not available or just don't understand.
But any time of the day or night, God is available and
willing to listen. Eventually, He will respond and give you
strength to carry on. You may need to turn away from
family and friends and turn only to Him. Be sure that your
tears are directed to the right one—God.

Soulful Affirmations

APRIL 24

~~~~~~

I manifest what I say.

—Juanita Payne

Matthew 21:22

"And all things, whatsoever ye shall ask in
prayer, believing, ye shall receive."

Do you know how powerful your words are? Everything
begins with a word. "In the beginning was the Word, and
the Word was with God, and the Word was God." Words
give life. If words are our beginning, let's use them to
believe and manifest the good we want.

APRIL 25

I am commissioned to focus on the water in MY cup.

—Yvette #theEXCHANGE McGill

Matthew 7:3 (NIV)

"Why do you look at the speck of sawdust in your brother's eye and pay no attention to the plank in your own eye?"

A lady in the church told the pastor she wasn't coming back because there were too many sinners. The pastor asked her to walk around the church twice with a cup of water. She had to report that she was so focused on the cup, she did not notice what anyone else was doing.

Soulful Affirmations

APRIL 26

~~~~~~

I am willing to see things differently.

—Dr. Sonya Wade Johnson

2 Corinthians 4:18 (NIV)

"So we fix our eyes not on what is seen, but
on what is unseen, since what is seen is
temporary, but what is unseen is eternal."

Every day seek to see things differently. It could be
something you often see that suddenly looks different.
When we allow God to use us in a way that manifests
newness, our lives are refreshed and we are transformed.

APRIL 27

~~~~~~

I invest in my goals and dreams.

—Yumica Thompson

Habakkuk 2:3 (NLT)

"This vision is for a future time. It describes the end,
and it will be fulfilled. If it seems slow in coming,
wait patiently, for it will surely take place."

How have you envisioned your life? When we are young, we
use our imagination to help make what seems impossible
possible. Examine your strengths, set goals, write down
your plan, develop your skills, and execute. The key to
success is trusting in God's promises and knowing that it is
not when you start . . . it's that you start.

Soulful Affirmations

APRIL 28

I am uniquely created.

−Vivian Grafton

Psalm 139:14

"I will praise thee; for I am fearfully and
wonderfully made: marvelous are thy works;
and that my soul knoweth right well."

Did you know that there is no one else in the world
just like you? Someone may look, sound, or walk like you
but there is only one you! God created you just as
He had in mind. Remember there is NOT another you.
How do you see yourself?

APRIL 29

~~~~~~

I am who God says I am.

—Tiffany Mayfield

Isaiah 43:1 (NIV)

"Do not fear, for I have redeemed you;
I have summoned you by name; you are mine."

The human mind is one of the most powerful
and inspirational tools we have. Our thoughts
shape who we become.

Remind yourself that you are created to be renewed in
the Spirit of God. Remind yourself that your identity does
not lie in your mistakes, your embarrassment, nor those
discouraging voices in your head or from others. You are
made in His image and likeness. You are given purpose
by God. You are blessed. You are provided for. You are a
believer. Believe in who He says you are and your purpose.

Soulful Affirmations

APRIL 30

I will change my life by changing my way of thinking.

—Taylor Spells

Isaiah 55:8 (NIV)

"'For my thoughts are not your thoughts, neither are your ways my ways,' declares the Lord."

Do you realize how powerful your thoughts are? What you think, you manifest into your life. We need to remember that thinking negatively will turn into speaking negatively. Our thoughts are not God's, but if we make His thoughts ours then things will shift. If we want to be like the Lord, then we must think like the Lord.

MAY 1

~~~~~~

I will hold on to God's promises.

—Sonya M. Hall-Brown

Hebrews 10:23 (ESV)

"Let us hold fast the confession of our hope without wavering, for he who promised is faithful."

Every promise of God is worth holding on to.
When God makes a promise, you can be certain He will fulfill it. When God makes a promise, He keeps it. The basis of our faith is God's faithfulness to fulfill His promise.
Are you holding on to God's promises?

Soulful Affirmations

MAY 2

~~~~~~

God is all I need.

—Joyce Brown, 2019 Ms. Texas Senior America

Revelation 22:13 (NIV)

"I am the Alpha and the Omega, the First and
the Last, the Beginning and the End."

What challenges are you facing—health concerns,
financial hardship, loss of a job? Know that God is
bigger than any challenges you face. He knows about
your challenges and He delights Himself in turning
your challenges into victories. Your challenges are the
steppingstones needed to build your character. It is only
in the challenging times that we develop the skills and
character needed to fulfill God's purpose for our life.

MAY 3

I will humble my hopes.

—Jenette Allen, EdS

Philippians 4:11 (NLT)

"Not that I was ever in need, for I have learned
how to be content with whatever I have."

God celebrates a child who can be humble in their
present circumstances. Can you see what you have as a
blessing and not focus on what you do not have? Situations
could always be worse! So, praise God for the little and
praise Him for the gain. If you can have faith to be content
when you lack, God will notice your humble spirit and
richly bless your faithfulness.

MAY 4

~~~~~~

*I will be honest with myself by looking into the mirror
to see how I contribute to my own destruction.*

—Janie Lacy

Haggai 1:5 (NIV)

"Now this is what the Lord Almighty says:
'Give careful thought to your ways.'"

Consider your ways. Are you optimizing your time,
talents, and gifts? Think about what is occupying most of
your day. Make the paradigm shift as you take inventory,
self-reflect, and focus on your shortcomings. Remember
that it is not always about what other people have
done to you. Own it! Destiny awaits!

MAY 5

~~~~~~

I will do it afraid.

—Heidi Lewis

Psalm 118:6 (BSB)

"The LORD is on my side; I will not be afraid."

How many times have you allowed fear to keep you from taking advantage of opportunities? Or how many times have you started something then fear talks you out of it? For some of us, our fear isn't that we'll fail. We know what failure looks like and we know how to get up. We fear success. Ask yourself, "If not now, when? If not now, why? If not me, who?" Everything you need is in you, so do it afraid.

MAY 6

~~~~~~

I will not worry over what I feel I can't control.

—Frances Ann Bailey

Philippians 4:6 (MSG)

"Don't fret or worry. Instead of worrying, pray.
Let petitions and praises shape your worries into
prayers, letting God know your concerns."

How many times have you felt a problem won't
get fixed unless you fix it? Do you know that God wants
you to rest in Him and allow Him to work on your behalf?
When you pray, you show God that you trust Him to fix your
issue and when you give praises, you are telling Him that
you believe that what you stand in need of is already done.
Worrying has no positive rewards. Don't stress
yourself out. Do it God's way.

MAY 7

~~~~~~

I am free to be who God created me to be!

—Fatima Williams

Ephesians 2:10 (ESV)

"For we are his workmanship, created in Christ
Jesus for good works, which God prepared
beforehand, that we should walk in them."

There are times when we shape our lives around
the desires and happiness of others and we often find
ourselves shackled, unhappy, and in circumstances or
places we were not meant to be. You were strategically
designed by God for a divine purpose. The only way you
can fulfill your purpose is to walk freely in your creative
design. There is no other you!

MAY 8

I am at rest in the finished works of Jesus.

−Dr. Angela Kinnel

Psalm 37:7 (NLT)

"Be still in the presence of the LORD, and wait patiently for him to act. Don't worry about evil people who prosper or fret about their wicked schemes."

Being at rest in the finished works of Jesus means that you understand that every obstacle you face was already handled on the cross. Jesus conquered every sin, obstacle, lack, hurt, and disappointment that comes into your life. As believers, we must apply our faith to what He has done.

MAY 9

~~~~~~

I believe in the sovereign God.

—Dr. Eric L. Holmes

Isaiah 50:7 (NLT)

"Because the Sovereign LORD helps me, I will not be dismayed. Therefore, I have set my face like a stone, determined to do his will. And I know that I will triumph."

God, you have been my source and my strength in the time of my weakness. You have allowed me to be victorious through every trial and storm I had to endure. I give you praise and glory because, with your help, I am determined to do your will for my life.

Soulful Affirmations

MAY 10

~~~~~~

I hide the Word of God in my heart.

—Melissa Shiver Sumpter

Psalm 119:11

"Thy word have I hid in mine heart, that
I might not sin against thee."

Think of something that's precious to you that you wouldn't
want anyone to steal. The Word of God is valuable.
It should be hidden in your heart so that the devil can't
steal it from you. The Word of God is a precious jewel!
It's more precious than silver or gold.

MAY 11

~~~~~~

I am empowered to win.

—Traci Henderson Smith

Ephesians 3:20

"Now unto him that is able to do exceeding abundantly
above all that we ask or think, according
to the power that worketh in us."

Do you put everything on God? Whether you win or lose,
succeed or fail? What about the goodness that manifests, or
doesn't, in your life? Thanks be unto God who is well-able
to bring you successes far more abundantly, beyond
anything you can ask for or think of, BUT it is according to
the power that is already working in you!

YOUR power activates HIS ability to help you win.

Soulful Affirmations

MAY 12

~~~~~~

I am watchful of my words before I speak.

—Danielle McGruder

Proverbs 15:4 (NIV)

"The soothing tongue is a tree of life, but a
perverse tongue crushes the spirit."

Once hurtful words have been spoken and an apology has
been accepted, the offended person may still feel the hurt
from those words, so please always be mindful of the words
spoken out of emotions. People may forgive, but they may
never forget how you made them feel in that moment.

Do you use a filter when speaking to others?

MAY 13

~~~~~~

I live in the power of peace.

—Danette M. Brown

Psalm 91:1 (NIV)

"Whoever dwells in the shelter of the Most High
will rest in the shadow of the Almighty."

How many times have you found yourself not taking
advantage of being a kingdom citizen of Heaven? How
often have you found yourself living in uncertainty and
unhappiness due to fighting your own battles? I have found
myself there several times, not living in God's fullness.
What is holding you captive that you need to let go and let
God handle to live in His peace?

MAY 14

I am whole even as I grow and heal.

—Cynthia Fox Everett

Acts 3:19 (NKJV)

"Repent therefore and be converted, that your sins may be blotted out, so that times of refreshing may come from the presence of the Lord."

Do you worry you will never be enough? You must tell yourself you aren't your negative thoughts or the thoughts of others. Healing is a process where nothing happens overnight. You have all you need inside of you, just activate it.

MAY 15

~~~~~~

I determine what I deserve and when I deserve to have it.

—Cynthia Drummond Andrews, MBA

Jeremiah 29:11 (NIV)

"'For I know the plans I have for you,' declares
the LORD, 'plans to prosper you and not to harm
you, plans to give you hope and a future.'"

We are moved by the Spirit. Put forth the effort
to treat everyone as you want to be treated. Do not allow
man to determine your worth, what you deserve to have,
and when you deserve to have it. Trust God to allow
your blessings to flow in His time.

Soulful Affirmations

MAY 16

~~~~~~

I will stop allowing doubt to creep into my mind when I pray to God.

—Contessah Irene Davis

Mark 11:24 (NASB)

"Therefore I say to you, all things for which you
pray and ask, believe that you have received
them, and they will be granted you."

Once you have made your request known to your
heavenly Father, write it down and begin to thank Him
for blessing you with what you have asked for, daily!
Remember that without faith it is impossible to please God.
So, first things first, trust God!

MAY 17

~~~~~~

I expect the best in life.

—Cheryl Polote-Williamson

3 John 1:2

"Beloved, I wish above all things that thou mayest prosper
and be in health, even as thy soul prospereth."

Expect to be blessed. Always. It is your reward as a
believer. Expect financial wealth. Expect good health.
Expect spiritual soundness and richness deep down in your
soul. Expect wholeness in your family, social, and business
relationships. Expect it. Expect the absolute best in life!

Soulful Affirmations

MAY 18

~~~~~~

I will serve today.

—Charlene E. Day

1 Peter 4:10-11 (NIV)

"Each of you should use whatever gift you have
received to serve others, as faithful stewards
of God's grace in its various forms."

My company works in partnership with corporations and
communities. When God first gave me the assignment to
create these projects, I was fearful. It involved me doing a
bulk of work. I made up in my mind... I will serve no matter
what. How are you being called to serve?

MAY 19

~~~~~~

I will praise until it breaks.

—Anitra Green

Acts 16:25

"And at midnight Paul and Silas prayed, and sang
praises unto God: and the prisoners heard them."

In life, we sometimes find ourselves in bondage to illness,
financial debt, or an unfavorable domestic situation.
Decide today that you will praise your way through it.
Like Paul and Silas, praise your way out of your prison;
out of bondage; through your midnight; and into your
new, victorious day. Praise God until you break through,
break out, and break free.

MAY 20

~~~~~~

*I am bold, beautiful, and brilliant in business, and
I attract multimillion-dollar contracts.*

—Anissa Green Dotson

Psalm 37:4 (NIV)

"Take delight in the Lord, and he will give
you the desires of your heart."

Your size does not matter. Degrees do not matter.
But faith does! Stand in the mirror and proclaim God's
Word over your business. His Word cannot return void.
I stepped out on faith, started my business, opened
accounts, and secured office space all before my
first contract. It's your time now!

MAY 21

~~~~~~

Today, I step into my purpose and my destiny.

—Angela Thomas

Proverbs 16:3 (NIV)
"Commit to the Lord whatever you do,
and he will establish your plans."

We often wonder what is our purpose and destiny?
Naturally, we have desires we think will bring fulfillment.
Be confident in who you are in Christ. Walk out your
purpose and trust His Word to be a lamp unto your feet
and a light unto your path. You will then discover your
strengths, passion, and purpose.

MAY 22

~~~~~~

I have confidence my heart's desires are favored by God.

—Alicia L. Hemphill

Esther 5:3 (AMP)

"What is troubling you, Queen Esther? What is your request? It shall be given to you, up to half of the Kingdom."

Many believers fear sharing what they want. Sometimes you hear them say, "God knows my heart." They avoid the challenging work of hope by avoiding disappointments due to delayed prayer. Can you begin to verbalize what you want? Speak of it often, knowing that it has already been granted to you.

MAY 23

~~~~~~

I am strengthened and renewed every day.

—Sandra Reese Jolla

Nehemiah 8:10

"The joy of the LORD is your strength."

Do you ever feel weak or like your strength is running out? Each day brings new life, new opportunities, and new challenges. Looking at the endless firmament of the heavens, the deeply planted roots of an old oak tree, or even the feathery wings of the birds as they soar across the clear blue sky gives me renewed hope and faith that my possibilities are infinite. I seek opportunities to make a difference each day at work, at home, or even on a casual walk in the park.

Soulful Affirmations

MAY 24

~~~~~~

I uniquely illuminate every room I walk into.

—Russell M. Williamson

John 1:5 (NLT)

"The light shines in the darkness, and the
darkness can never extinguish it."

Every one of us has been endowed with a certain
set of talents. While they may seem similar to someone
else's, they are uniquely woven together by our Abba Father.
He knew us before we were born and knitted us
together in our mother's womb. Our unique gifts are a
brilliant light that God asks us to shine for His glory.
Let your light shine everywhere you go.

MAY 25

~~~~~~

The peace of God resides in me.

—Dr. Sheila Bunton

John 14:27(a) (NIV)

"Peace I leave with you; my peace I give you.
I do not give to you as the world gives."

The peace of God is a free gift for anyone who is
willing to accept it. It is a gift that aids and strengthens
us during life's most challenging times. God's peace is
reserved for those who are bold enough to receive it,
and it is patient enough to wait on those who have yet to
obtain it. Which one are you? What adjustment, if any,
do you need to make for peace?

MAY 26

~~~~~~

I am not in competition with anyone except myself.

−Dr. Peggie Etheredge Johnson

Galatians 6:4 (NASB)

"But each one must examine his own work, and
then he will have reason for boasting in regard to
himself alone, and not in regard to another."

Are there times and circumstances that trigger personal
examination and comparison of your life to others,
producing thoughts that perhaps they have greater
advantages with God than you? These feeling often
produce negative comparisons, jealousy, and cynicism.
Your time and energy are wisely spent discerning God's
accomplishments in you as He expands your capacities.
Compliment others as you challenge yourself!

MAY 27

~~~~~~

I give myself permission to forgive.

—Juanita Payne

1 Peter 4:8 (NIV)

"Above all, love each other deeply, because
love covers over a multitude of sins."

Do you know that when you choose to forgive it
frees you? It's not just simply saying, "I forgive you."
Instead, it is not holding on to the reason why you
do not want to forgive, making a conscious decision
to let go of negative feelings, and forgiving.

MAY 28

~~~~~~

I will use moments of trouble and despair to
build my character and inspire others.

—Chartonna "CeCe" Woodley

2 Corinthians 4:16-18 (NLT)

"That is why we never give up. Though our bodies are dying, our spirits are being renewed every day. For our present troubles are small and won't last very long. Yet they produce for us a glory that vastly outweighs them and will last forever. So, we don't look at the troubles we can see now; rather, we fix our gaze on things that cannot be seen. For the things we see now will soon be gone, but the things we cannot see will last forever."

It is tempting to get stuck in a negative mindset when trouble arrives. I challenge you to journal through the storm and prepare for the sun to shine.

MAY 29

~~~~~~

I am resilient.

—Danielle McGruder

Psalm 145:14

"The Lord upholdeth all that fall, and raiseth
up all those that be bowed down."

When you have resilience, you bounce back after all trials,
tribulations, and heartaches. Sometimes God makes us
uncomfortable to stretch us to our full potential. You keep
moving on, no matter how hard it may look. It may not be
easy but in the end, with God as your guide, the storms will
be worth going through. How do you bounce back when
you are taken out of your comfort zone?

MAY 30

~~~~~~

I accomplish all of my goals on time without procrastinating.
—Tammy L. Woodard

Ephesians 5:15-16 (NIV)

"Be very careful, then, how you live—not as unwise but as wise, making the most of every opportunity, because the days are evil."

When you say, "I will do it tomorrow," you take time for granted. I can't tell you how many times I have missed opportunities due to procrastination. Tomorrow is not promised. Make today a priority. Don't waste time on things that don't matter. You are the only person standing in the way of your success. Take immediate action.

MAY 31

~~~~~~

I am millionaire minded.

−Shameka Oliver

3 John 1:2 (NKJV)

"Beloved, I pray that you may prosper in all things
and be in health, just as your soul prospers."

A millionaire mindset, the very act of focusing on your
money, will dramatically improve the decisions you make.
Wealthy people who invest more time into planning their
finances invariably make better decisions, get better
results, and achieve financial independence.

JUNE 1

~~~~~~

I attract God-inspired ideas that produce millions of dollars.

—Cheryl Polote-Williamson

Proverbs 22:29 (NIV)

"Do you see someone skilled in their work? They will serve before kings; they will not serve before officials of low rank."

Stop saying you don't know how. You do know. Profess now that you have the mind of Christ. Your eyes are enlightened; your mind is open. You receive daily downloads of fresh and innovative ideas that will bring you wealth.

JUNE 2

~~~~~~

I am looking to the Lord for strength. I will move accordingly.

—Lynder E. Scott, MBA

1 Chronicles 16:11 (NIV)

"Look to the LORD and his strength;

seek his face always."

Would you like to know how to get your prayers
answered? I think I heard a yes. You will get your prayers
heard and answered by God through a relationship
with Him. That relationship requires continuous
communication, worshipping Him, honoring Him,
and loving Him; moreover, trusting Him. Please
know that God does consider your request and He
truly knows what is best. No matter what, trust His
response. That is the highest form of worship.

Soulful Affirmations

JUNE 3

~~~~~~

I will listen.

—Charlene E. Day

Revelation 3:20 (NIV)

"Here I am! I stand at the door and knock. If anyone
hears my voice and opens the door, I will come in
and eat with that person, and they with me."

Listen closely to your heart. God is giving you
instructions. Doctors use stethoscopes to clearly hear
the rhythm of the heart . . . what's good or bad. My
ultimate desire is for you to get good at listening to
God so that you can hear what is good for your life.

JUNE 4

I will learn to pick my battles wisely.

—Cynthia Fox Everett

Exodus 14:14 (ESV)
"The LORD will fight for you, and
you have only to be silent."

We are taught to fight and defend our family and
property, but when we have to totally trust God it can
be exhausting and challenging. He will give you wisdom
and strength to trust His abilities and your own.

JUNE 5

~~~~~~

I will complete my tasks.

—Dr. Sheila Bunton

Isaiah 43:2 (NIV)

"When you pass through the waters, I will
be with you; and when you pass through the
rivers, they will not sweep over you."

How many people do you know or have you encountered
that rarely complete a task? How many people do you know
that start out excited only to lose their momentum? Are
you one of them? On our journey, we will encounter many
challenges and obstacles. While we go through them, we
will discover that God was with us every step of the way.

What assignments do you need to complete today?

JUNE 6

~~~~~~~~~~~~~~~~~~~~~~~~~~~~~~~~~~~~

I keep going because I am fully covered.

—Chartonna "CeCe" Woodley

Daniel 3:25 (NLT)

"'Look!' Nebuchadnezzar shouted. 'I see four men, unbound, walking around in the fire unharmed! And the fourth looks like a god!'"

During the times you thought you would not survive, God was right there making a way. You are protected. Even in the darkest hour, the light is on the way. Affirm His Word, stand on it, and repeat it daily while you are awaiting a breakthrough.

JUNE 7

~~~~~~

*I will take responsibility for my peace and do
what is necessary to maintain it.*

—Contessah Irene Davis

Isaiah 26:3 (NASB)

"The steadfast of mind You will keep in perfect
peace, Because he trusts in You."

Establish a continuous chat between yourself and the Lord
throughout your day and you'll find your mind at ease even
when the world around you isn't. Keep your mind on God,
knowing His mind is on you, and watch how His peace will
overtake you and be perfected within you.

JUNE 8

~~~~~~

I wake up every day knowing that I will receive powerful blessings.

—Cynthia Drummond Andrews, MBA

Hebrews 11:6 (NIV)

"And without faith it is impossible to please God, because anyone who comes to him must believe that he exists and that he rewards those who earnestly seek him."

Every day is a new day to embark upon growth, success, wealth, happiness, and all the desires of your heart. It all begins with faith and expectations! Expect your blessing today! God knows the desires of your heart. When you walk in expectation, truly believe, and you are patient, you will receive all the desires of your heart.

JUNE 9

~~~~~~

I have faith when speaking victory over my storms.

—Danielle McGruder

Isaiah 43:2 (NIV)

"When you pass through the waters, I will be with you;
and when you pass through the rivers, they will not
sweep over you. When you walk through fire, you will
not be burned; the flames will not set you ablaze."

While praising God amidst trouble, we find ourselves
surrounded by peace that may not make sense, but it will
change our outlook of that situation. No matter how you
feel, God will hold you together. How will you motivate
others while they are amid a storm?

JUNE 10

I will embrace adversity.

—Denise Polote-Kelly

James 1:2-3 (NIV)

"Consider it pure joy, my brothers and sisters, whenever you face trials of many kinds, because you know that the testing of your faith produces perseverance."

Difficulties are opportunities for growth and personal development. Whenever trouble comes, we should consider it an opportunity for joy. When your faith is tested, remember that it is a chance for you to grow and let God take control. God will protect you from your adversities and give you the strength to go through them.

JUNE 11

~~~~~~

I give myself grace.

—Shaundre Emmerson

Romans 14:22 (NIV)

"Blessed is the one who does not condemn
himself by what he approves."

Are you feeling guilty due to work, children, and
everyday stresses? Are you consumed with fixing
everything, then something goes wrong? Do you think,
*Is it me or is it just fate? Why did I do that? What could
I have done to avoid this? It's all my fault.* You are doing
the best you can with what you're working with. Don't be
so hard on yourself. God's grace is sufficient.

JUNE 12

~~~~~~

I refuse to lose my joy!

—Melissa Shiver Sumpter

Romans 12:12 (NIV)

"Be joyful in hope, patient in affliction, faithful in prayer."

Whatever you do, don't lose your joy in hope!
Are you under attack by the enemy or just going through
a hard test from the Lord? While going through the
process, don't lose your joy in hope. Use your weapon
of prayer during difficult times.

JUNE 13

I am learning to trust the process although I do not understand it.

—Tiffany Mayfield

Ecclesiastics 8:6 (NASB)

"For there is a proper time and procedure for every delight, though a man's trouble is heavy upon him."

God wants you to know that He is preparing you for what He wants to do through you. The process is teaching you to trust Him. Be bold in your faith, character, and gifts.

The process brings the promise.

Preparation must come before opportunity.

Trust the process.

It is bringing His promises to fruition.

JUNE 14

~~~~~~

I am strong and courageous.

—Deborah A. Smith

Joshua 1:9 (NIV)

"Have I not commanded you?
Be strong and courageous."

Being afraid, fearful, and weak at times is never a good feeling. Just know that GOD has your back. He is with you when you travel through the highways and byways. The journey may be long, but GOD is holding your hand every step of the way. There is no need to be fearful, afraid, or weak. You are strong and courageous.

Soulful Affirmations

JUNE 15

~~~~~~

I will not let anxiety control my thoughts and waste my time.

—Taylor Spells

Matthew 6:27 (NIV)

"Can any one of you by worrying add
a single hour to your life?"

Do you benefit from being anxious and afraid? Anxiety is when you are depleted of faith and not able to let God do His work. Being anxious and worrying does nothing but take time off of our lives. God wants us to place our fears onto Him and let Him take care of things. Therefore, ask yourself, "Should I worry or should I pray?"

JUNE 16

~~~~~~

I live a Godly life so that I can have a purposeful life.

—Sandra Reese Jolla

Psalm 1:1a (NKJV)

"Blessed is the man Who walks not in
the counsel of the ungodly."

Do you feel good when you do the right thing?
How do you know what is right? Living and applying
Godly principles enables me to live my life to the fullest.
Understanding my spiritual gifts and talents helps me to
navigate God's direction for me. I am allowing God's Word,
instead of worldly yearnings, to direct and guide me.
He assures me that despite life's trials, I am walking in
His unfolding plan for me.

JUNE 17

I am an encourager.

—Myoshi Robinson Thomas

1 Thessalonians 5:11 (NIV)

"Therefore encourage one another and build
each other up, just as in fact you are doing."

God wants us to uplift, encourage, and motivate
each other to become positive and productive. He wants
us to walk in our purpose and help others cross over
the bridge to success. I was told that there is a
superpower within all of us. What is yours?

JUNE 18

~~~~~~

I change my mindset to change my behavior to change my outcome!

—Necole Martinez

Roman 12:2 (ESV)

"Do not be conformed to this world, but be transformed by the renewal of your mind, that by testing you may discern what is the will of God, what is good and acceptable and perfect."

Have you ever wanted a different result but didn't know where to start? Have you ever wanted change but didn't know how to make it happen? Everything starts in the mind. God can help us transform our outcomes by helping us to transform our mindset. When we start to see things in a positive light, positive things happen.

JUNE 19

~~~~~~

God is my protector.

—Dr. Eric L. Holmes

2 Thessalonians 3:3

"But the Lord is faithful, who shall stablish
you, and keep you from evil."

We face many trials and circumstances as we journey
through life, but what is most certain is that God is our
keeper and protector. No matter what has happened in our
lives, our God has been a refuge and strength who keeps
watching over us. He said that He would never leave us nor
forsake us. He is a keeper of His word.

JUNE 20

~~~~~~

My actions will always lead to rewards.
—Yvette #theEXCHANGE McGill

Galatians 6:9 (NIV)

"Let us not become weary in doing good, for at the proper time we will reap a harvest if we do not give up."

One night, I prayed so hard about a matter that I made myself sick. Then, God woke me up in the middle of the night and directed me to the above Scripture. The moment I turned my faith toward good things, good things came toward me. HIS Word can't return void.

JUNE 21

~~~~~~

I will trust God until the vision comes to pass.

—Melissa Powell-Harrell

Genesis 21:1 (NIV)

"Now the LORD was gracious to Sarah as he had said,
and the LORD did for Sarah what he had promised."

The vision will tarry, but it will come to pass at
the right time. We must maintain hope during trouble,
doubt, and when it seems like the vision will not come to
pass. God is faithful and will bring His promise to pass.
Celebrate all victories with God.

JUNE 22

~~~~~~~~~~~~~~~~~~~~~~~~~~~~~~~~~~~~~~~

I make it happen.

—Traci Henderson Smith

2 Timothy 1:7 (NIV)

"For the Spirit God gave us does not make us timid,
but gives us power, love and self-discipline."

Built within you is what it takes to make
things happen. Power, a sound mind, and no fear to
approach tasks are your birthright. So, when you feel
fear creeping in, do it scared and the fear will bow down
to you. Boldly walk in the authority and dominion
that causes things to go well for you.

JUNE 23

~~~~~~

I will stay firm in my faith.

—Sonya M. Hall-Brown

1 Corinthians 15:58 (NKJV)

"Therefore, my beloved brethren, be steadfast, immovable, always abounding in the work of the Lord, knowing that your labor is not in vain in the Lord."

God calls you to be firm and unchanging in your faith. Every day, you face spiritual attacks. From the world that would say you are foolish to believe to the forces of darkness that try and discourage you, your faith is always being tested. Are you staying firm in your faith?

JUNE 24

~~~~~~

I will no longer dwell on my past mistakes.

—Frances Ann Bailey

2 Corinthians 5:17 (NLT)

"This means that anyone who belongs to Christ has become a new person. The old life is gone; a new life has begun!"

What do you do when someone tries to remind you of your past? You then remind them who you belong to. Enjoy your new life in Christ and refuse to dwell on who you used to be. God has allowed every mistake to shape and mold you into who you are today. If you remember anything, remember that your past worked or is working for your good.

JUNE 25

~~~~~~

I accept new roles and titles as new chapters unfold.

—Chartonna "CeCe" Woodley

John 9:25

"He answered and said, Whether he be a
sinner or no, I know not: one thing I know,
that, whereas I was blind, now I see."

Your new role will make some people wonder,
How in the world? People may question your position or
authority, but just remember that you were chosen.
At your next level, surround yourself with winners and
people who are where you want to be. Explain yourself to
no one and give the credit to the Creator.

JUNE 26

~~~~~~

I matter.

—Juanita Payne

1 Peter 2:9 (NIV)

"But you are a chosen people, a royal priesthood,
a holy nation, God's special possession, that you
may declare the praises of him who called you
out of darkness into his wonderful light."

Did you know that you matter? God predestined you before
the foundation of the world. Stop letting people define who
you are. God created you for a purpose and on purpose.
Yes, you were chosen by Him to do great and marvelous
things. Tell yourself today, "I matter."

Soulful Affirmations

JUNE 27

~~~~~~

My gift is needed in the earth.

—Vivian Grafton

1 Timothy 4:14

"Neglect not the gift that is in thee, which was
given thee by prophecy, with the laying
on of the hands of the presbytery."

We all have been given a gift that we really love doing.
That gift gives us a sense of fulfillment like nothing else.
Have you been using it, perfecting it, investing into it?
If not, why not start today? Otherwise, you are
denying the earth what you have inside of you.

JUNE 28

~~~~~~

I will have hope in everything God has given me to do.

—Meyett Lavalais

Romans 15:13 (NASB)

"Now may the God of hope fill you with all joy
and peace in believing, so that you will abound
in hope by the power of the Holy Spirit."

Hope is God's gift created specifically for you.
When life is dark, just know that Jesus carried the cross,
bearing all the burden for you to have joy, peace, and hope.
This is His gift to you.

Soulful Affirmations

JUNE 29

~~~~~~

I make a conscious decision to protect my peace at all cost.

—Tammy L. Woodard

John 14:27 (NIV)

"Peace I leave with you; my peace I give you.
I do not give to you as the world gives."

God has given us a helper that dwells in us—
the Holy Spirit. He also gave us another gift. We
often say, "Lord, give me peace." Jesus has already
provided us with peace, we just need to tap into
it. Choose peace and protect it at all cost.

JUNE 30

I am not afraid because God is leading the way.

—Russell M. Williamson

Deuteronomy 31:8 (NLT)

"Do not be afraid or discouraged, for the Lord
will personally go ahead of you. He will be with
you; he will neither fail you nor abandon you."

There are days when you feel all alone and you wish there
was someone to help, someone else to fix it, or someone
else to pay. Fear is not your friend, but faith is. Replace fear
with faith because this path has been traveled before by
God. He is with you, and with God you win in the end.

JULY 1

~~~~~~

*I will work at remaining humble no matter how
much I acquire or achieve in life.*

—Contessah Irene Davis

Deuteronomy 8:18 (NASB)

"But you shall remember the Lord your God,
for it is He who is giving you power to make
wealth that He may confirm His covenant which
He swore to your fathers, as it is this day."

When you've accomplished success, it can become
difficult to remain humble, especially when you are around
those who do not operate in humility. Remember that
the Lord is the source and sustainer of your success.
Keep that in the forefront of your mind, always.

JULY 2

~~~~~~

I never think that part of me is lacking or that I am less than.

—Cynthia Fox Everett

Genesis 1:27 (NKJV)

"So God created man in His own image; in the image of God He created him, male and female He created them."

God is always in motion towards us. He is working with us where we are. Trust in His power to change us daily into His image. We don't have to be perfect, just willing. God knows that we are imperfect, and He loves us anyway, just like we are.

JULY 3

~~~~~~

I walk in the protection of wisdom.

—Deborah. A. Smith

Ecclesiastes 7:12 (NIV)

"Wisdom preserves those who have it."

Wisdom is free and available to help you make the right decisions. When it comes to your finances, gaining knowledge, or taking care of your family, ask GOD for the protection of wisdom today. You will make smart moves in all that you do because you have the protection of wisdom.

JULY 4

~~~~~~

I am limitless!

—Cynthia Drummond Andrews, MBA

Isaiah 41:10 (NIV)

"So do not fear, for I am with you; do not be dismayed,
for I am your God. I will strengthen you and help you;
I will uphold you with my righteous right hand."

"I can't" does not exist. The only limitations you have in life
are those things that you resist. You can do whatever you
desire. Fear is only a state of mind. Let go of the fear of the
unknown and allow God to bless you. Release the fears of
the unknown and walk by faith.

Soulful Affirmations

JULY 5

~~~~~~

My tears will be worth it.

—Dr. Eric L. Holmes

Psalm 126:5

"They that sow in tears shall reap in joy."

Many times, we have cried about things that have happened in our lives. One thing I am reminded of is that tears can be viewed from another perspective. Just know that though we have cried, those tears are bringing about great joy. So, cry, then turn around and laugh.

JULY 6

~~~~~~

I have authority over the spirit of fear.

—Dr. Angela Kinnel

Psalm 118:6 (NLT)
"The LORD is for me, so I will have no fear.
What can mere people do to me?"

Fear is the nemesis of faith. Have you ever had a dream
to accomplish a goal, but you didn't pursue it due to fear
of failure? Walking in fear contaminates your faith. As
believers, we have the spiritual authority to speak over
ourselves. We have been given the right to command what
we want under God's power through grace. So when fear
starts to raise its ugly head, we must decree and declare,
"No fear here, in Jesus' name!"

Soulful Affirmations

JULY 7

~~~~~~

I will stretch beyond my place of comfort.

—Fatima Williams

1 Corinthians 9:24 (ESV)

"Do you not know that in a race all the runners run, but only one receives the prize? So run that you may obtain it."

Have you ever wondered if there is more in life for you or if you can possibly reach a higher mark? It is human nature to enjoy comfort; however, we should never be complacent. Stretch to enlarge your territory, stretch to go higher, and stretch to win!

JULY 8

~~~~~~

*I will grieve and not ignore or bottle up my
heartbreak so that I can heal.*

—Janie Lacy

Proverbs 13:12 (NIV)

"Hope deferred makes the heart sick, but
a longing fulfilled is a tree of life."

Anchor yourself in dignity so that you don't have to try
to perform CPR on a situation that coded. When you do
this, you grieve privately, and you don't vent your emotions
publicly on social media. You must cast your cares on God
who will provide counsel so that you can heal.

Soulful Affirmations

JULY 9

~~~~~~

I turn my worries over to God and He gives me peace.

—Joyce Brown, 2019 Ms. Texas Senior America

Mathew 11:28 (NIV)

"Come to me, all you who are weary and
burdened, and I will give you rest."

What are you worried about? Finances? Children?
Your job? Your spouse? Worrying creates stress and steals
your peace. Worry leads to unhealthy habits like alcohol,
drugs, overeating, etc. In prayer, give God your problems
and allow Him to intercede on your behalf. God wants
to take full control of your life. When you give your cares
to Him, you will find peace during your storm. What
challenges are you ready to give up?

JULY 10

~~~~~~

I will plan based on proper preparation.

—Denise Polote-Kelly

Jeremiah 29:11 (NIV)

"'For I know the plans I have for you,' declares
the LORD, 'plans to prosper you and not to harm
you, plans to give you hope and a future.'"

How often have you made plans to take a trip, make
a purchase, begin a relationship, join a congregation,
etc.? It is important for us to make plans but never to be
presumptuous about anything. Seek God first in all that you
do, for He will direct your path. Plan, then seek God
for the answers as you move.

Soulful Affirmations

JULY 11

*God is enlarging my territory because I have
been faithful over what He has given me.*

—Frances Ann Bailey

Matthew 25:23 (NIV)

"His master replied, 'Well done, good and faithful
servant! You have been faithful with a few things;
I will put you in charge of many things. Come
and share your master's happiness!'"

Have you ever thought that whatever you are doing needs
to be better or that it just isn't good enough? Do you know
that God isn't looking for you to be perfect over what you
have but to remain loyal over what He has given you?
When God sees that He can trust you with the little and
you remain steadfast, He will increase you to handle more.
Don't be hard on yourself, just continue to give God a return
on His investment and get ready for expansion.

JULY 12

~~~~~~

I inspire industrious impossibilities.

—Jenette Allen, EdS

Hebrews 11:6

"But without faith it is impossible to please him: for he that cometh to God must believe that he is, and that he is a rewarder of them that diligently seek him."

Nelson Mandela said, "It always seems impossible until it's done." This quote is powerful because it speaks to the achievement of insurmountable feats. God guides us to have faith when we are surrounded by challenging circumstances. Without faith, we cannot please Him nor can we be successful! Today, despite the challenge, have faith, please God, and achieve something impossible!

Soulful Affirmations

JULY 13

~~~~~~

Wealth comes to me in miraculous ways.

—Cheryl Polote-Williamson

2 Corinthians 8:9 (ASV)

"For ye know the grace of our Lord Jesus Christ, that,
though he was rich, yet for your sakes he became poor,
that ye through his poverty might become rich."

Define your expectations and set the stage now for how
you desire to be blessed. As a believer, your rebirth right
is wealth—wealth in family and relationships, wealth in
gifts and talents, wealth in your bank account. Please
understand that you have a biblical right to wealth in all
areas—mind, body, soul, and finances.

JULY 14

~~~~~~

I am not forgotten.

—Heidi Lewis

Genesis 16:13a (NIV)

"She gave this name to the LORD who spoke to her:
'You are the God who sees me.'"

How many times have you made decisions without consulting God, only to be disappointed when your plans didn't work? It seems as if God isn't answering your prayer or He doesn't understand. It's in those times that we have to realize that He's working in the background, destroying the traps we didn't see and causing our names to be spoken in rooms we thought we'd never sit in. He's heard your prayers and He hasn't forgotten you.

Soulful Affirmations

JULY 15

~~~~~~

I partake in the fountain of youth daily.
Therefore, I will be young forever.

—Tanya M. Turner

Psalm 92:14 (NIV)
"They will still bear fruit in old age,
they will stay fresh and green."

Did you know that health is the new wealth?
Yes, investing in our health is one of the best investments
we can ever make. When we focus on our overall well-being
and incorporate self-care routines into our daily lives,
we extend love and appreciation to ourselves.
What is your favorite self-care routine?

JULY 16

~~~~~~~~~~~~~~~~~~~~~~~~~~~~~~~~~~~~~~~

Every opportunity afforded me will be used to share what is true.

—Yumica Thompson

Colossians 1:29 (NIV)

"To this end I strenuously contend with all the
energy Christ so powerfully works in me."

The smallest embellishment is misleading. People should
never second-guess what you share with them or your
presentation of information. A good story changes over
time. A true story stands the test of time. Be intentional
when sharing evidence with others. What you do and say
can draw people closer to God or lead them away from
Him. When in doubt, the Word of God is the best reference.

Soulful Affirmations

JULY 17

~~~~~~

I am the perfect image of my Creator!

—Tammy L. Woodard

Genesis 1:27 (NIV)

"So God created mankind in his own image, in the image of God he created them; male and female he created them."

Everything that God created is perfect. You were purposely designed in the image of God. You are fearfully and wonderfully made. You don't need to change a thing. You are beautiful in every way. No matter your body type, height, or complexion, you are uniquely designed. Love and accept every inch and difference in yourself.

JULY 18

~~~~~~

I build strong relationships through collaboration.

—Tangie Barkley Robinson

Proverbs 27:17 (ESV)

"Iron sharpens iron, and one man sharpens another."

Have you ever played a team sport in school? Did you enjoy the camaraderie? We can take that same team sport philosophy and apply it to every area of our lives to build strong relationships. Working together will give you a sense of accomplishment, support, and partnership. I challenge you to create your winning team for every area of your life.

JULY 19

~~~~~~

I will fast and pray often.

—Sonya M. Hall-Brown

2 Chronicles 20:3-4 (NKJV)

"And Jehoshaphat feared, and set himself to seek the
LORD, and proclaimed a fast throughout all Judah. So,
Judah gathered together to ask help from the LORD; and
from all the cities of Judah they came to seek the LORD."

This past year and a half, I was in a dark place.
The glow I once had was gone. The Bible teaches us that
we must fast often and pray in times of distress. God is the
only one that can deliver us from those gloomy days.
Have you tried fasting and praying?

JULY 20

~~~~~~

It's in my DNA to be successful.

—Yvette #theEXCHANGE McGill

Jeremiah 1:5 (NIV)

"Before I formed you in the womb I knew you,
before you were born I set you apart;
I appointed you as a prophet to the nations."

I used to feel tied up in sin's bed. I used to think the
generational flaws inherited through my family had tracked
me down. But then I remembered that Christ won. Back at
Calvary, HE interrupted my blood line, rewrote my DNA,
changed my name, and gave me HIS identity.
I'm now known as a curse breaker.

Soulful Affirmations

JULY 21

~~~~~~

I will not allow anyone to make me feel invisible or unimportant.

—L. Lorraine Hale-Cooper

Romans 2:1

"For there is no respect of persons with God."

They counted you out—again! It may seem as if you
try and try but people put you in a box and overlook your
gift. Just know that box they see as plain and simple,
others (the right ones) will soon see as a beautiful
GIFT box. Don't allow anyone to keep you from
using the talent God gave you. His gifts are for us all.
Are you ready to shine and be received?

JULY 22

~~~~~~

I will choose to stop procrastinating.

—Juanita Payne

Galatians 6:9

"And let us not be weary in well doing:
for in due season we shall reap, if we faint not."

Do you find yourself saying, "I wish I had more time
to get things done" or "I feel like I do not have enough
time to do anything." Why do we put off what can be
accomplished today until tomorrow? God has blessed
us with 24 hours a day. I challenge you to act today.

Soulful Affirmations

JULY 23

~~~~~~

My presence enhances every situation, and my gifts are needed.
—Traci Henderson Smith

Matthew 5:16

"Let your light so shine before men, that they may see your good works, and glorify your Father which is in heaven."

The ability to make things better is woven into the fabric of your being. Your mere presence enhances every situation. You are a light. You shine bright. You are a blessing to every team, project, and assignment. You must believe and confess this without arrogance and pride, but with humility, assurance, and readiness to take every vision to the next level. Making a difference is your superpower and the world is lucky to have you!

JULY 24

~~~~~~

I am confident, competent, and credible.

—Lashunda Denby

Proverbs 22:1 (NIV)

"A good name is more desirable than great riches;
to be esteemed is better than silver or gold."

Confidence, competence, and credibility demands
intelligence and skill, which results in specific knowledge
of how to get the job done and provides good service or a
quality product. Think about those qualities, be honest with
yourself, then answer this question: If you wouldn't hire
yourself, then why do you think someone else would?

JULY 25

I will talk about ideas, not gossip about people.

—Dr. Madge L. Barnes

Ephesians 4:29 (ESV)

"Let no corrupting talk come out of your mouths, but only such as is good for building up, as fits the occasion, that it may give grace to those who hear."

Gossip is an easy trap in which to be caught. Sometimes, it is under the guise of concern. Gossip is hurtful to all involved, even the bearer. We can learn to recognize it, stop it, and move on to another subject or person. How can you make your conversations count today? If heard, how can you end gossip today?

JULY 26

~~~~~~

I use my authority to advocate for others.

—Meyett Lavalais

Lamentations 3:34-36 (CSB)

"Crushing all the prisoners of the land beneath one's feet, denying justice to a man in the presence of the Most High, or subverting a person in his lawsuit— the Lord does not approve of these things."

With authority comes great responsibility which coincides with Luke 12:48. We are all a part of the kingdom of God, and those who have been tasked with great power have a specific directive given by Him to advocate for those in need.

JULY 27

~~~~~~

I will live a life of peace.

—Tara Johnson

John 14:27 (NIV)

"Peace I leave with you; my peace I give you.
I do not give to you as the world gives.
Do not let your hearts be troubled and do not be afraid."

God wants us to live in peace. So often, we worry about
unnecessary things that we have no control over. The
opinions or standards of others is not your main concern.
Find peace and worth within yourself and stop allowing
fear to stand in the way of your heart's desires.

JULY 28

~~~~~~

I will strive to bring peace into my life and my soul.

—Taylor Spells

Isaiah 32:17 (NIV)

"The fruit of that righteousness will be peace;
its effect will be quietness and confidence forever."

Does your soul feel at rest or is it disturbed? The Lord
wants you to trust Him to bring peace into your life. Peace
within is when the storm inside of you has been silenced.
When we have faith in God, He will reward us with peace
in our life and calmness will prevail.

JULY 29

~~~~~~

I will use my push to conquer my fears.

—Marsha Taylor

Psalm 42:11

"Why art thou cast down, O my soul? and why art thou disquieted within me? hope thou in God: for I shall yet praise him, who is the health of my countenance."

Standing at my window watching the rain pour down on the windowpane broke my inner silence. The silence of prolonged fears and uncertainties of the future turned into an unexpected reassurance that came from hearing the laughter of my children as they ran through the house with their happy-go-lucky spirits. I embrace those thoughts of fear; I know what real push is! I will never give up! You can never give up. We will pray for it until it happens.

JULY 30

~~~~~~

I am the Creator's masterpiece.

—Tiffany Mayfield

Ephesians 2:10 (NLT)

"For we are God's masterpiece.
He has created us anew in Christ Jesus, so we can
do the good things He planned for us long ago."

It is true—you are a masterpiece. Not because of how
healthy, accomplished, or politically correct you are.
You are a masterpiece because of what God has done in
your life by grace and by your identity in Christ.
This is true no matter how you feel today.

I challenge you to know God's truth and live in it.
You are His masterpiece.

Soulful Affirmations

JULY 31

~~~~~~

My faith triumphs over my fear.

—Sandra Reese Jolla

Psalm 27:1 (NIV)

"The LORD is my light and my
salvation—whom shall I fear?"

Have you ever received news that numbed you? Your
heart started racing and fear completely overcame you?
Because God is my guiding light, I have no reason to fear.
The prophet Isaiah tells us: "No weapon formed against
you shall prosper, and every tongue which rises against
you in judgment you shall condemn." The Lord's presence
reassures me that I can be safe even when I am fearful.
When I am overcome with fear, I take a deep breath and
remember that faith gives me strength to overcome fear.

AUGUST 1

~~~~~~

I release all of my limiting beliefs.

—Renee Denise Fowler

2 Corinthians 10:5 (NASB)

"And we are taking every thought captive
to the obedience of Christ."

We all have limiting thoughts. Limiting thoughts
are beliefs that are destructive to our success.
Awareness is the first step to eradicating limitations.
If you remain unaware, you won't know what to adjust.
The Message Bible says, "We use our powerful God-tools
for smashing warped philosophies, tearing down barriers
erected against the truth of God." Use the tools you have
been given to smash limiting thoughts and to create
new thoughts, habits, and behaviors.

AUGUST 2

~~~~~~

I am making moves my children's children will thank me for.
—Yvette #theEXCHANGE McGill

Psalm 100:5 (NIV)

"For the LORD is good and his love endures forever;
his faithfulness continues through all generations."

On the night of my mom's funeral, GOD said to me,
"If you want your funeral story to be different, you must
do something different now, Yvette." I'm commissioned
to do just that every day, which is why I pray for GOD to
make up the difference where I fall short. When GOD is
for you, who can be against you?

AUGUST 3

~~~~~~

I am content in my place of peace.

—Danielle McGruder

John 14:27

"Peace I leave with you, my peace I give unto you:
not as the world giveth, give I unto you.
Let not your heart be troubled, neither let it be afraid."

I pray daily for God to cover me with a sense of peace that
surpasses all understanding and to give me a sense of
security that I have longed for my entire life. Peace fills me
with strength that carries me through each day with new
mercies. How does peace make you feel?

AUGUST 4

~~~~~~

I will bless your name, mighty God.

−Dr. Eric L. Holmes

Job 9:10

"Which doeth great things past finding out;
yea, and wonders without number."

God, you have been so faithful to cover and restore me.
You have kept me from dangers seen and unseen. When
I consider how great You are, I bless Your name and give
You the glory. In the midst of it all, You remain faithful and
mighty. Your greatness is unsearchable and there is no
one like You. Thank You for being so mighty in my life and
allowing me to share with the world that You are great.

AUGUST 5

~~~~~~

I am greater than my worst mistake.

—Traci Henderson Smith

Philippians 3:13 (NLT)

"No, dear brothers and sisters, I have not achieved
it, but I focus on this one thing: Forgetting the
past and looking forward to what lies ahead."

Don't allow anyone to hold you bondage to your past.
Captivity is not God's plan for you. You are greater than
that. You are forgiven. Forgive yourself and reach with
everything in you towards your bright
and prosperous future.

Soulful Affirmations

AUGUST 6

I have the favor of God.

—Sonya M. Hall-Brown

Proverbs 12:2

"A good man will obtain favor from the LORD, But
He will condemn a man who devises evil."

If you are like me, you want to live in the favor and
blessings of God. I want to experience everything God
has for me. I don't want to get to Heaven and find out
that I missed out on most of God's blessings. I want to
receive every blessing God wants me to have.
Do you want the favor of God?

AUGUST 7

I believe in myself even when no one else does.

—Tammy L. Woodard

Philippians 1:6 (NIV)

"Being confident of this, that he who
began a good work in you will carry it on to
completion until the day of Christ Jesus."

You are your biggest advocate! As you navigate
through life and pursue your dreams, you'll find that others
may not see your vision. The people that you think
will support you, most likely will not. Don't let that
discourage you! Encourage yourself and believe that
God created you for greatness!

AUGUST 8

~~~~~~

I settle and submit to God.

—Anitra Green

James 4:7

"Submit yourselves therefore to God.
Resist the devil, and he will flee from you."

I know what you're thinking, and you are wrong.
Submit is not a bad word, it is a powerful word.
Settle into the thought that what God wills for you may
not be what you want for you. Settle down and
submit to His will for your life.

When a person can submit their will and ways to the will of
the Lord, that is powerful. Settle and submit to Him.

AUGUST 9

I will use my voice.

—Charlene E. Day

Isaiah 58:1

"Cry aloud, spare not, lift up thy voice like a trumpet."

When you are doing God's will, there will be
situations that will cause you to feel like no one hears you.
You will feel like you've been muted.

How has the enemy attempted to mute you?
Check your surroundings.

Check yourself. Don't stop using your voice.
Cry out even louder!

Soulful Affirmations

AUGUST 10

~~~~~~

I cherish the memories and keep the faith.

—Angela Thomas

Matthew 5:4 (NIV)

"Blessed are those who mourn, for they will be comforted."

Did I ever imagine that he would leave me first? I thought it would be me who left him. Unanswered questions, anger, blame, hurt, and sadness. In the room but not present. Walking but in a daze. Flawed but my angel. He made me laugh and he made me proud. As a believer, despite the emptiness, I trusted God; He lifted me. For us, He sacrificed His only begotten Son. I take solace in knowing my son is safe. Cherish the memories and keep the faith.

AUGUST 11

~~~~~~

I will live confidently in God's promise.

—Dr. Madeline J. Anderson Thomas

Psalm 23:6

"Surely goodness and mercy shall follow me all the days of
my life: and I will dwell in the house of the LORD for ever."

The world is constantly changing. You have God's promise
to be with you always and the assurance of His goodness
and mercy. Your relationship with God is marked by His
favor and the blessed effects of it. God's abundant love,
goodness, and mercy will pursue you for your entire life.

AUGUST 12

~~~~~~

I am confident knowing that fierce faith falsifies fear.

—Jenette Allen, EdS

2 Timothy 1:7

"For God hath not given us the spirit of fear; but
of power, and of love, and of a sound mind."

Have you ever had a moment when you needed to move
or act, but you felt idle? Was it fear of the unknown that
kept you immobile? When you feel like you can't handle the
pressure to take the first step, lift up your head,
lift up your eyes, muster all of your faith (even if it is
as small as a mustard seed), and trust God!

Cheryl Polote-Williamson   230

AUGUST 13

I will let go of the grudge.

—Denise Polote-Kelly

Matthew 18:21-22 (NIV)

"Then Peter came to Jesus and asked,
'LORD, how many times shall I forgive my brother or sister
who sins against me? Up to seven times?' Jesus answered,
'I tell you, not seven times, but seventy-seven times.'"

Wow! How do we forgive a person 490 times?
Jesus stands up for us over and over again asking God to
forgive us. What if God had only forgiven us once? None of
us would be here. Whatever the situation, forgive and let
go so that you can live and love completely. Sometimes you
have to forgive without closure.

AUGUST 14

~~~~~~

I will not allow outside turbulence to disturb my peace.

—Fatima Williams

Philippians 4:6-7 (NKJV)

"Be anxious for nothing, but in everything by prayer and supplication, with thanksgiving, let your requests be made known to God; and the peace of God, which surpasses all understanding, will guard your hearts and minds through Christ Jesus."

There are times when you are in a place of peace then you look up and you have an incoming bomb heading your way. We cannot allow that outside interference to push us from that place of assurance. We must know, through all of the turbulence, that our God is in control! Trust Him during chaos and remain steady in peace.

AUGUST 15

I work towards building wealth today.

—Deborah A. Smith

Proverbs 10:4 (NIV)

"Lazy hands make for poverty,
but diligent hands bring wealth."

Make every moment and opportunity that comes your
way today count. Think about the one goal you have been
planning to accomplish for years but never acted on. Are
you fed up with not having enough? GOD has given you the
strength to build wealth. Get busy and bring in the wealth
that your diligent hands can help you achieve.

Soulful Affirmations

AUGUST 16

*I succeed and prosper and am in good
health, just as my soul prospers.*

—Dr. Angela Kinnel

3 John 1:2 (AMP)

"Beloved, I pray that in every way you may succeed
and prosper and be in good health [physically], just
as [I know] your soul prospers [spiritually]."

Success happens when a purpose or aim is
accomplished. To prosper is to thrive physically in good
health and have all needs met. We have a blood-bought
right to succeed in every area of our lives. Be sure that
living words flow out of you. A good place to start is by
declaring the Word of God over yourself.

AUGUST 17

~~~~~~

I will pray, wait, and make sound decisions.

—Janie Lacy

Psalm 37:4 (NIV)

"Take delight in the LORD, and he will
give you the desires of your heart."

Would you be in your current situation if you had listened
to God? Have you governed your decisions based upon your
flesh? It is important to evaluate your present attractions.
Immaturity and physicality will have you wasting time
entertaining the wrong people. Ask yourself,
"Am I becoming who I desire to be spiritually?"

Soulful Affirmations

AUGUST 18

I choose forgiveness.

—Heidi Lewis

Ephesians 4:32

"And be ye kind one to another, tenderhearted,
forgiving one another, even as God for
Christ's sake hath forgiven you."

Have you ever heard someone say, "I'll forgive, but I'll
never forget"? How often have you said the same thing?
Are you waiting for an apology that you may never receive?
Forgiving someone isn't about them, it's about you. You
aren't responsible for what the other person does, you
are responsible for what you do. Healing begins with the
decision to forgive. How can you receive forgiveness if you
won't give it? I challenge you to choose forgiveness.

AUGUST 19

~~~~~~

I honor yesterday because I am in love with today!

—Necole Martinez

Romans 15:4 (NASB)

"For whatever was written in earlier times was written for our instructions, so that through perseverance and the encouragement of the Scriptures we might have hope."

How many times have we looked back at our past and asked God, "Why me?" How many times have we tried to cover up our negative experiences because of guilt and shame? Everything we've experienced has been a steppingstone to the very thing we have asked for from God. Lessons learned give us hope for a better tomorrow and light for the present day. God gives us adverse experiences to help grow and mold us into the vision He has for us. When we look back at our past, it gives us hope for a better tomorrow because we have overcome yesterday!

Soulful Affirmations

AUGUST 20

~~~~~~

*I will actively listen when communicating
with people to get understanding.*

—Tangie Barkley Robinson

Proverbs 18:2 (ESV)

"A fool takes no pleasure in understanding,
but only in expressing his opinion."

Have you ever had a conversation with someone and you
were quick to respond without fully understanding their
message? I challenge you today to be fully present in the
conversation. Pay attention to their facial expressions,
body language, tone of voice, and the speed at which they
talk to get understanding. What are they really saying?
What is the unspoken message? We all can become better
communicators by listening.

AUGUST 21

~~~~~~

I will purposefully spread joy.

—Yumica Thompson

Proverbs 17:22 (NLT)

"A cheerful heart is good medicine,
but a broken spirit saps a person's strength."

We've all faced trials, tribulations, traumas, and grief.
While in the midst of tragedy, confusion, and dismay,
do not allow the joy given to you by the Lord to diminish.
During such occasions, laugh more, sing more,
and praise God for all He has done. May the joy of
the Lord strengthen you, always.

Soulful Affirmations

AUGUST 22

I am in control of my peace.

—Juanita Payne

John 14:27 (NIV)

"Peace I leave with you; my peace I give you.
I do not give to you as the world gives.
Do not let your hearts be troubled and do not be afraid."

Who or what is robbing you of your peace?
God wants us to take hold of the peace that He has given
us, no matter what's going on around us. Continue
to seek His face. I challenge you to pray about
everything and worry about nothing.

AUGUST 23

*My current situation has to change and is
suddenly changing right now!*

—Frances Ann Bailey

1 Peter 5:10 (NIV)

"And the God of all grace, who called you
to his eternal glory in Christ, after you have
suffered a little while, will himself restore you
and make you strong, firm and steadfast."

How many times have your circumstances made
you think that God has forgotten about you or that maybe
He is punishing you? Do you know that God loves you so
much that He will take you out of things you put yourself
into? He even made you a promise that your suffering has
an expiration date. You have to know and believe,
by faith, that what you are in right now will soon
end and restoration is on its way.

AUGUST 24

~~~~~~

I let go so I can grow.

—Dr. Sheila Bunton

Proverbs 4:25 (NIV)

"Let your eyes look straight ahead;
fix your gaze directly before you."

It is impossible to look forward while looking backward. In order to move forward, one must be willing to let go and fix their eyes on what lies ahead. God has given us the ability and power to let go of things that rendered us powerless and broken. It is God's will to lead us throughout life's journey. What things do you need to let go of? What things are causing you to look backward versus moving forward?

AUGUST 25

I am not compromising my spiritual immune system with hatred.

—Dr. Peggie Etheredge Johnson

Acts 17:26a, 28c (NKJV)

"And He has made from one blood every
nation of men to dwell on all the face of the
earth . . . we are also His offspring.'"

Do you struggle with loving and treating others justly
because they do not look or act like you? The spirit of
hatred poisons and lingers in the heart to instigate a
rollercoaster of negative emotions, irrational biases,
stereotypical opinions, and bondage that obstructs the
spirit of love needed to manifest the freedom to
patiently love and forgive God's family.

AUGUST 26

~~~~~~

*I have access to all the tools I need to have
a successful and thriving business.*

—Tanya M. Turner

Psalm 115:14 (NIV)

"May the LORD cause you to flourish,
both you and your children."

We live in an uber driven society. It is imperative that
we gain access to the tools needed for our businesses to
thrive in a competitive environment. Being a good steward,
learning your craft, and knowing your market, along with
continuous growth and development are keys to evolving
and flourishing long-term.

AUGUST 27

~~~~~~

I fear not. I am the courageous person God said I am.
—Joyce Brown, 2019 Ms. Texas Senior America

Joshua 1:9 (NIV)

"Be strong and courageous. Do not be afraid;
do not be discouraged, for the LORD your
God will be with you wherever you go."

Many entertainers experience stage fright, others
experience the fear of public speaking. What are your
fears? Fear can paralyze you. It will prevent you from
accomplishing your goals and stunt your growth.
God wants us to face fear head on. Move forward despite
the fears you are experiencing. Challenge yourself,
accomplish those uncomfortable tasks, and lean on
God's strength to see you through.

Soulful Affirmations

AUGUST 28

~~~~~~

In my suffering, I will rest on the things above.

—Michelle Franklin

Colossians 3:1-2

"If ye then be risen with Christ, seek those things which are above, where Christ sitteth on the right hand of God. Set your affection on things above, not on things on the earth."

Looking above towards Heaven reminds me that I am not my circumstances. Coming into a place of freedom is work and it's my choice. God doesn't force me to look up and trust Him. I must fight to align my vision with the things above. There lays my rest.

AUGUST 29

~~~~~~

I control what I dump into my trash can.

—Nina Gaddie Howard

Romans 8:28 (NIV)

"And we know that in all things God works
for the good of those who love him, who have
been called according to his purpose."

Choose what you will hold on to, reflect on, or trash.
You have no space to allow other's negativity and drama to
fill the needed space in your own trash can. After prayer,
meditation, and reflection, let go, empty your trash
can, and start the new day.

AUGUST 30

~~~~~~

I am invigorating my mind with optimistic words.

—Myoshi Robinson Thomas

John 1:1 (AMP)

"In the beginning (before all time) was the
Word (Christ), and the Word was with God,
and the Word was God Himself."

Have you ever thought about the words you speak
and how they trigger your mind? The things we speak
shape our mind. Each word should draw a beautiful picture
of what you want to see. Today, choose to invigorate your
mind with positive and encouraging words that will
shape your day, future, and life.

AUGUST 31

~~~~~~

My past hurts will not determine my future.

—Royleta Foster

Jeremiah 30:17 (NKJV)

"For I will restore health to you And heal you of your wounds,' says the LORD, 'Because they called you an outcast saying: 'This is Zion; No one seeks her.'"

Have you ever felt a hurt that you thought you could never get past? God does not want our past holding us back. It is ok to forgive yourself and others. God loves you and wants you to be successful because you are His child. Allow God to heal your hurts.

SEPTEMBER 1

I am chosen and called into God's royal priesthood.
—Bishop Richard S. Johnson

1 Peter 2:9 (NKJV)

"But you are a chosen generation, a royal priesthood,
a holy nation, His own special people, that you
may proclaim the praises of Him who called you
out of darkness into His marvelous light."

Has anyone said you were worthless or good for nothing?
Did you subscribe to their hypothesis and suppositions?
God alone can justly say who you are and what you will
become. Others may have preconceived ideas of your
worth, but God doesn't honor their assessments so why
should you? You are called royalty. Believe God!

SEPTEMBER 2

~~~~~~

My prayers are powerful.

—Sonya M. Hall-Brown

James 5:16 (NASB)

"Therefore, confess your sins to one another, and pray
for one another, so that you may be healed. The effective
prayer of a righteous man can accomplish much."

Prayer is a powerful weapon. When you pray,
you connect with God and release the power of Heaven
into your situation. Through prayer, people have been
saved, healed, and transformed. Do you believe in
what you are praying for?

Soulful Affirmations

SEPTEMBER 3

~~~~~~

I speak life. I am healed.

—Tara Johnson

Proverbs 18:21 (NIV)

"The tongue has the power of life and death,
and those who love it will eat its fruit."

How often do we think the worst of a diagnosis or
situation? We go straight to the worst case scenario
or outcome for our life. But there is so much power
in what we speak over ourselves. The more we voice
negativity, the more we are claiming it; whereas,
a positive heart speaks positive words. Continually speak
life, healing, and growth over yourself and your family.
Start today and confess, "I am healed."

SEPTEMBER 4

~~~~~~

I will check my treasure box.

—Anitra Green

Colossians 2:3

"In whom are hid all the treasures
of wisdom and knowledge."

In earthly treasures, you expect to find jewels, gold, and
money, none of which will get you into Heaven. These
things are only of good to you here on Earth. But in
heavenly treasures, you find peace, joy, wisdom, knowledge,
and most importantly, eternal life. Check your treasure box
and ensure it is filled with heavenly treasures.

Soulful Affirmations

SEPTEMBER 5

I hear you God. Your voice WINS, every time!
—Yvette #theEXCHANGE McGill

Psalm 27:8 (NKJV)

"When You said, 'Seek My face,' My heart said
to You, 'Your face, LORD, I will seek.'"

One of the few things I now know I cannot live without is
hearing from GOD on a daily basis. My first experience
hearing from Him was during a very low moment in my
young adult life. I will never forget it as long as I live.

SEPTEMBER 6

I exude and attract positive energy.

—Tammy L. Woodard

Psalm 19:14 (NIV)

"May these words of my mouth and this meditation of my heart be pleasing in your sight, LORD, my Rock and my Redeemer."

Make a conscious decision to steer away from negativity. This may mean changing your circle, mindset, and habits. A simple smile can change the way you look and the way people perceive you. Thinking good thoughts about yourself will build your confidence and make others take notice. Positive thoughts and actions produce positive results.

SEPTEMBER 7

~~~~~~

*I receive all of God's instructions because
His plan for me has no limitations.*

—L. Lorraine Hale-Cooper

Luke 1:37

"For with God nothing shall be impossible."

Have you ever had an idea and happily shared it with someone only to be told, "You can't do that." Well, if God put it in your spirit, won't He give you everything you need to succeed? Be careful who you allow to influence you. Fast, pray, and seek God for yourself. Is there someone you need to drop as God takes you to your mountain top?

SEPTEMBER 8

~~~~~~

I am an advocate.

—Shameka D. Johnson

Proverbs 31:8-9 (NIV)

"Speak up for those who cannot speak for themselves,
for the rights of all who are destitute. Speak up and
judge fairly; defend the rights of the poor and needy."

Whether family, friend, or stranger . . . sometimes we
need to be the voice for those that are unable to speak
for themselves. It is up to us to take a stand for those that
cannot. Being silent is being part of the issue.
Who will you be an advocate for today?

Soulful Affirmations

SEPTEMBER 9

The wisdom God gives me will lead to the road less traveled.

—Yumica Thompson

Matthew 7:14 (AMP)

"But small is the gate and narrow and difficult to travel is the path that leads the way to [everlasting] life, and there are few who find it."

When the Holy Spirit provides guidance, will you follow? There will come a time when you must separate yourself from negativity to stay focused on your path. Learn to say no to people and things that dissuade you from getting closer to God. Be confident in the plans He has for you.

SEPTEMBER 10

I intentionally speak to people in a positive tone of voice.

—Tangie Barkley Robinson

Proverbs 15:4 (ESV)

"A gentle tongue is a tree of life,
but perverseness in it breaks the spirit."

How we speak to someone sets the tone for how they will receive and respond to our message. The tone of our voice affects the outcome of the message. How the message is relayed can either uplift or tear down. We all have to be mindful of our tone with each other to get our point across and to be heard. What tone of voice will you use today?

Soulful Affirmations

SEPTEMBER 11

God's illumination is my greatest tour guide.

—LaToya Adams

Psalm 119:105 (NKJV)

"Your word is a lamp to my feet And a light to my path."

Illumination grants access to wisdom and awakens our consciousness to follow the plan created for us. Each step taken according to God's Word will illuminate our path and guide us even through the darkness designed to lead us astray.

SEPTEMBER 12

I will always trust my Owner's Manual (Bible) for solutions.

−Dr. Madge L. Barnes

Hebrews 13:8

"Jesus Christ the same yesterday, and to day, and for ever."

Do you believe God is still working on your behalf for good? Yes, He is. You can rest assured that He has not forgotten you. God has not changed His mind about you because you made a mistake. He has the same plans that will enable you to succeed. The facts may appear contradictory to the truth, but God does not change. Rest in His assurance to bless you and bring you out on time.

Soulful Affirmations

SEPTEMBER 13

I will create a life for myself that is full of wealth and prosperity.

—Taylor Spells

Psalm 37:4 (NIV)

"Take delight in the LORD, and he will
give you the desires of your heart."

Do you want to be rich or do you want to be wealthy? God does not want us to focus on being rich financially, but to be abundantly wealthy in all areas of our lives. If being rich is a goal, then let it be your soul that is full of richness. Enjoy life with the Lord and you will have a life worth living.

SEPTEMBER 14

~~~~~~

I invest and manage my money wisely.

−Cheryl Polote-Williamson

Proverbs 21:20

"There is treasure to be desired and oil in the dwelling of the wise; but a foolish man spendeth it up."

Don't fall victim to wasting your money or allowing yourself to be cheated in frivolous ventures. Be wise and diligent in your pursuits. Make viable contacts and connections. Vet, vet, vet! Trust God to speak to you regarding what you should and should not do with your finances. At the same time, don't be afraid of money—making it or letting it go. Be a giver, a wise but cheerful giver, and watch God handle the rest.

Soulful Affirmations

SEPTEMBER 15

~~~~~~

My investments serve me with maximum returns.

—Roni Benjamin

Isaiah 30:23 (ESV)

"And he will give rain for the seed with which you sow the ground, and bread, the produce of the ground, which will be rich and plenteous. In that day your livestock will graze in large pastures."

Employ your money to work for you twenty-four hours a day. The question I have for you is, "Will you outlive your legacy, or will your legacy outlive you?" Some of the money you earn should be multiplied and continue to follow the sun all around the world.

SEPTEMBER 16

*I am building my businesses so that I can support
my divine assignment and worthy causes.*

—Michelle Winfield Fuqua

2 Corinthians 9:7 (WEB)

"Let each man give according as he has
determined in his heart; not grudgingly, or under
compulsion; for God loves a cheerful giver."

What do you classify as your business? Your business
can include employment and entrepreneurship. Working
just for a paycheck may not bring you satisfaction or
abundance. When you apply the principle of giving, the flow
of resources to you and from you grows in accordance
with your generosity. Deciding to give consistently
enriches your financial ecosystem.

SEPTEMBER 17

I will invest time to focus on my business plan and my legacy.

—Natasha M. Harris

Habakkuk 2:2

"And the Lord answered me, and said,
Write the vision, and make it plain upon
tables, that he may run that readeth it."

Have you desired to have your own business?
Do you have a service that you know without a doubt would
do well if you focused on putting your vision on paper?
The time is now. If you honor God through your
business, He will direct your path.

SEPTEMBER 18

I will continue to invest in my growth.

—Shameka D. Johnson

Romans 12:2 (NIV)

"Do not conform to the pattern of this world,
but be transformed by the renewing of your mind."

Being stagnant is not an option. Continued learning
expands the mind to create new ideas, new experiences,
and more. Investing in yourself allows for a beautiful
payout when least expected. Growth allows you into
new arenas and elevates you to a different playing field.
Growth opens you up to truly see the worth and
value you bring to the table. Read something that
aligns with where you see your future self.

Soulful Affirmations

SEPTEMBER 19

~~~~~~

I am wealthy in every way.

—Shameka Oliver

Deuteronomy 8:18

"But thou shalt remember the LORD thy God:
for it is he that giveth thee power to get wealth,
that he may establish his covenant which he
sware unto thy fathers, as it is this day."

God gives us the tools needed to be wealthy. We just have to
be faithful and believe in Him and we'll receive.

SEPTEMBER 20

~~~~~~

My storm has ceased; the sun shines.

—Shaundre Emmerson

Psalm 145:18 (NIV)

"The LORD is near to all who call on him."

Have you ever felt like what else can go wrong? What else can I lose? WHY ME? Sometimes we forget that God is with us even when we feel alone, struggling to survive. When you hit rock bottom, that's when you rely on the strength you've always had. Our brokenness gives us COURAGE to be vulnerable. To cry out to God and say, "Help me." Instead of asking, "WHY ME," say, "Why not me?" Thank you, LORD, for the storm!

Soulful Affirmations

SEPTEMBER 21

~~~~~~

I will speak life into dead situations, and things shall live again.

—Melissa Powell-Harrell

Proverbs 23:7

"For as he thinketh in his heart, so is he:..."

Words have power over us and others. I believe all thoughts manifest at some level in our lives. Words have the power to bring things into existence. They have the power to change people, places, and things. I will use my words to create and build, not to tear down.

SEPTEMBER 22

I will speak blessings over this generation and the next.

—Meyett Lavalais

Psalm 33:11 (CSB)

"The counsel of the Lord stands forever, the plans of his heart from generation to generation."

There is nothing that will exist outside of God's sovereignty. He knows all that was created and anything that will be cultivated for the future. It is all within His reach. There is nothing God cannot touch.

SEPTEMBER 23

~~~~~~

I will step back from my own thoughts and trust God.

—Janie Lacy

Proverbs 3:5 (NIV)

"Trust in the LORD with all your heart and
lean not on your own understanding."

I trust You, God, and refuse to participate in a
system that says, "You've got to make things happen
because your time is running out." Father, I am content in
You and trust that as the divine potter, You will mold
and make me out of Thy will.

Are you trusting Him based on your
behavior or His will?

SEPTEMBER 24

~~~~~~

I am a peacemaker.

—Russell M. Williamson

Psalm 34:14b (NIV)

"Seek peace and pursue it."

Having a space that allows you to attain physical and mental peace is invaluable. Take a moment to be still and quiet your mind. Welcome the Lord in and embrace the moment because He longs to spend time with you.

SEPTEMBER 25

~~~~~~

I get stronger with every test.

—Minister Kiesha L. Peterson

Galatians 6:9

"And let us not be weary in well doing:
for in due season we shall reap, if we faint not."

How long have you been in your season of tests? I can only
imagine. I know it feels like this season never goes away.
You may not feel it, but your tests and trials really do come
to make you stronger. God does not allow things to happen
to wipe you out, He allows them to happen to make you
stronger. How will you use your test results?

SEPTEMBER 26

*I declare and decree that the chaos and
confusion of this world will not destroy me.*

—Michelle Franklin

Proverbs 4:23

"Keep thy heart with all diligence;
for out of it are the issues of life."

It is my responsibility to guard my heart and mind each
day. Yes, God has given me the strength to endure. I
acknowledge that my will is more powerful than my flesh.
When I have it under control, peace will be my portion
because I will command my flesh to surrender.

SEPTEMBER 27

I will protect my peace.
—Shawntelle Y. Jones

Daniel 10:19 (NIV)

"'Do not be afraid, you who are highly esteemed,'"
he said. "'Peace! Be strong now; be strong.'"

God will not put more on you than you can bear. How do
you stay at peace? Do you like listening to music? Do you
pray about it? Do you go for a long walk or drive? God
wants His children to be at peace and to come to Him
when the stress of everyday life is too much to handle.
What are you doing to protect your peace?

SEPTEMBER 28

~~~~~~

I will lead the way with resilience and compassion.
To my frontline health care heroes.

—Sherry Wurgler

Joshua 1:9 (NIV)

"Have I not commanded you? Be strong and courageous.
Do not be afraid; do not be discouraged, for the LORD
your God will be with you wherever you go."

Did your past tell you that you weren't enough?
Are you living with doubt and uncertainty?
The truth is you have a heart of gold!
You are more precious than silver!
Your touch is helping to heal wounds.
Your smile is bringing warmth to a sterile hospital setting.
Your compassion is giving hope to those
feeling lost and hopeless.
Your devotion and dedication are breathing
life and sustenance into hundreds of thousands
of patients around the globe.
You are not alone!
We all stand together!
Your life matters!

SEPTEMBER 29

I can fight injustice with Heaven's angel armies.

—Alicia L. Hemphill

Matthew 18:15 (NIV)

"'If your brother or sister sins, go and point out
their fault, just between the two of you. If they
listen to you, you have won them over.'"

Do you feel dread and anxiety when confronting
someone who has wronged you? Many believers fear strong
reactions when bringing correction to a brother or sister.
God expects believers to handle their relationships with
honesty, love, and conviction. How can He use you
to stop another's bad behavior?

SEPTEMBER 30

I spend time in the presence of God every day.

—Michelle Winfield Fuqua

Jeremiah 29:12-13 (WEB)

"You shall seek me, and find me, when you
search for me with all your heart."

Do you know that God does not hide from you? He is your
source for everything you need. For maximum results,
prioritize prayer as a daily, necessary practice. Prayer
consists of soaking and saying. Soaking allows you to rest
in His presence while saying allows you to offer
praises and petitions.

OCTOBER 1

~~~~~~

I am established in righteousness.

−Dr. Angela Kinnel

Isaiah 54:14 (AMP)

"You will be firmly established in righteousness:
You will be far from [even the thought of]
oppression, for you will not fear, And from
terror, for it will not come near you."

Do you know that you are the righteousness of God?
Once you accepted Jesus Christ as your Lord and
Savior, the gift of righteousness became available to you.
Righteousness does not come through your works. It
comes from adding your faith to what is available to you
through Jesus. It is yours! Receive it today!

OCTOBER 2

I will activate my faith over fear.

–Danette M. Brown

2 Timothy 1:7 (NKJV)

"For God has not given us a spirit of fear, but of
power and of love and of a sound mind."

Even in a season of sickness and disease, life can bring a
lot of uncertainty, a new normal, and distress to our lives
through the spirit of fear. As believers, we activate our faith
and stand on God's powerful words of having a mind like
Christ. What are you doing in this season to be at peace
with God's protection over your life?

OCTOBER 3

~~~~~~

My potential to succeed is infinite, and my success is limitless.

—Marie Hart

Romans 1:19-20 (NASB)

" . . . he who comes to God must believe that He is and that He is a rewarder of those who seek Him."

You will always face challenges. When you find happiness in the success, you will strive deeply to achieve more. Continue to build on that success with trust and faith in God.

OCTOBER 4

~~~~~~

I will rise above my circumstances today and dismiss the distractions.

—Marsha Taylor

Philippians 3:8 (NLT)

"Yes, everything else is worthless when compared with
the infinite value of knowing Christ Jesus my Lord.
For his sake I have discarded everything else, counting
it all as garbage, so that I could gain Christ."

Some of the circumstances that confront us are
meant to bring about our growth, not our failure.
I am reminded of the day I stopped to ask God, "Why me?"
His simple answer resonated with me when
He said, "It's not that serious!"
He was really saying, "Relax, it's just a distraction.
I have already won the battle for you!"

OCTOBER 5

*I will accept the fact that things may not always go my way, and
I will embrace and accept the next level GOD is taking me to.*

—Chartonna "CeCe" Woodley

2 Corinthians 4:8-9 (NLT)

"We are pressed on every side by troubles, but we are
not crushed. We are perplexed, but not driven to despair.
We are hunted down, but never abandoned by God.
We get knocked down, but we are not destroyed."

What is bothering you and keeping you up late at night?
What situation do you see no way out of? Where is hope
escaping you? I challenge you to see things in a different
light. See where the new journey may be leading you.

OCTOBER 6

~~~~~~

I am resilient and living proof of God's Grace.

—Angela Thomas

Jeremiah 17:14 (NIV)

"Heal me, LORD, and I will be healed; save me and
I will be saved, for you are the one I praise."

Why do we stay quiet? Why are we ashamed?
Just when I thought life's struggles, setbacks, and physical
challenges were the end of me, resilience kicked in and
gave me hope. The wilderness was dark and the ocean
swallowed me up, but God came down and delivered me.
I cried to God and He heard me. Your story may not
be my story, but it is a story that you survived.

Soulful Affirmations

OCTOBER 7

~~~~~~

I am an overcomer of loss, by faith.

—Natasha M. Harris

1 John 5:4 (NIV)

"For everyone born of God overcomes the world. This is the victory that has overcome the world, even our faith."

Being an overcomer can be a blessing to others when you are able to share your story in the form of a testimony. I encourage you to share your seed of inspiration. It could encourage others to overcome their obstacles by staying connected to their faith.

As we encourage, we're encouraged.

OCTOBER 8

I am not having an identity crisis.

—Bishop Richard S. Johnson

2 Corinthians 5:17 (NKJV)

"Therefore, if anyone is in Christ, he is a
new creation; old things have passed away;
behold, all things have become new."

Are you struggling to remain the same? Acceptance of
Christ as Lord, Redeemer, and Savior enters you into the
process of becoming His new creation. The new birth
should result in an innovative life in Christ. Your struggle is
real but submitting to God's transformation will introduce
you to a victorious life on Earth that extends to
eternity with God in Heaven.

Soulful Affirmations

OCTOBER 9

~~~~~~

I will forgive myself.

—Ruby Jeanine Batiste

1 John 1:9 (NIV)

"If we confess our sins, he is faithful and just and will forgive us our sins and purify us from all unrighteousness."

Upon accepting Jesus Christ as Lord and Savior, we become new creations. Sure, we will continue to stumble, but we must learn to forgive ourselves as we strive to be more like Him. What steps will you take today to forgive yourself for past sin?

OCTOBER 10

I will not live in fear.

—Sonya M. Hall-Brown

Isaiah 12:2 (ESV)

"Behold, God is my salvation; I will trust,
and will not be afraid; for the LORD GOD is my strength
and my song, and he has become my salvation."

Since God is your salvation, there is never a reason to live
in fear. He gives you strength in the midst of a fearful world.
I no longer live in fear. Do you?

OCTOBER 11

Mistakes and tragedy do not extinguish God's original plan for my life.
—Traci Henderson Smith

Psalm 37:24

"Though he fall, he shall not be utterly cast down:
for the Lord upholdeth him with his hand."

Mistakes and tragedy do not remove God's original
intentions for you. No matter what happened, God fully
expects His promises concerning you to come to pass.
There may be pain as a result of decisions you made or
things that happened, but you will still do the work He
called you to, walk in the purpose He laid out for you, and
have the life He promised you if you believe and act on His
promises. Your circumstances may have changed, but you
still have the power to win!

OCTOBER 12

~~~~~~

I will serve through the pain.

—Shameka D. Johnson

Philippians 4:13 (EHV)

"I can do all things through Christ, who strengthens me."

When grief takes ahold of your heart, it's as if your life
is completely depleted. Having the mindset that there is
always someone in a worse situation than you helps to
keep things in perspective. No, it does not remove the grief,
but it's a reminder to hold your head a little higher. Giving
to others with time, energy, and care has the capacity to
fill the hole caused by that grief. Serving is undoubtedly a
reward that God can give you the strength for.

Soulful Affirmations

OCTOBER 13

~~~~~~

I will show compassion to others.

—Melissa Shiver Sumpter

Ephesians 4:32 (NIV)

"Be kind and compassionate to one another, forgiving each other, just as in Christ God forgave you."

Can you remember a time when you asked the Lord to forgive you for something? Think of how you may have pleaded for His forgiveness. What if He didn't forgive you? Having compassion softens the heart to allow forgiveness of others. Try it, it really works!

OCTOBER 14

I will let Scripture shape my thoughts.
—Dr. Madeline J. Anderson Thomas

Proverbs 4:23 (NCV)

"Be careful what you think, because
your thoughts run your life."

Your thought life determines your actions. What you focus on will determine where you'll go. You will be all that God purposed and destined you to be when you elevate your mind daily with His Word. Today, will you be intentional in allowing God's Word to establish your mindset?

Soulful Affirmations

OCTOBER 15

*I am eating healthy. It compliments my amazingly
loving and contagious personality.*

—Lynder E. Scott, MBA

1 Corinthians 6:19-20 (NIV)

"Do you not know that your bodies are temples of the
Holy Spirit, who is in you, whom you have received from
God? You are not your own; you were bought
at a price. Therefore honor God with your bodies."

Are you making self-care a priority? For those that do,
awesome. The ones who haven't yet, your body is not yours.
It is on loan from God. Show Him daily how much you
appreciate your earth suit by having a healthy body.

OCTOBER 16

~~~~~~

My family is medicine-free and healthy.

—Shawntelle Y. Jones

3 John 2 (NLT)

"Dear friend, I hope all is well with you and that you
are as healthy in body as you are strong in spirit."

God is a healer, but He does not want you to
take your body for granted. He has blessed you with
great doctors and medicine to heal your body, but you
should do your best to remain healthy. What are you
going to do to remain healthy and medicine free?
What unhealthy choices will you change?

OCTOBER 17

~~~~~~

I will persevere and carry on.
To my frontline workers.

—Sherry Wurgler

Isaiah 40:31 (NIV)

"But those who hope in the LORD will renew their
strength. They will soar on wings like eagles; they will
run and not grow weary, they will walk and not be faint."

Yes, we are tired.
It's been a long journey.
We have learned.
We have grown deeper roots from the inside out.
We have grown stronger and more resilient that
we ever thought we could be.
Our journey is not yet over.
The battle still rages.
We have what it takes, and we will measure up
to whatever the future holds.
We will see this through until a cure is found.
You are beautiful and loved beyond belief.
We are all in this together, no one is alone!
We will stand together, strong as one!

OCTOBER 18

~~~~~~

I am saved and will always be saved!

—Yvette #theEXCHANGE McGill

John 10:28 (NIV)

"I give them eternal life, and they shall never perish;
no one will snatch them out of my hand."

Like many, I have experienced some really dark moments
in life; however, I always have just enough hope in me to
remember that I'm saved, I'm saved, I am SAVED. And at
the end of this journey, that's all that really matters.

OCTOBER 19

I always finish what I start with excellence.

—Shameka Oliver

2 Corinthians 8:11 (ESV)

"So now finish doing it as well, so that
your readiness in desiring it may be matched by
your completing it out of what you have."

The prophet Daniel lived an incredible life that was
marked with success and favor at every turn. Daniel
was preferred above the presidents and princes
because an excellent spirit was in him.

OCTOBER 20

~~~~~~

I spend and save money wisely.

—Roni Benjamin

Isaiah 55:2 (NWT)

"Why do you keep paying out money for what is not bread, And why spend your earnings for what brings no satisfaction? Listen intently to me, and eat what is good, And you will find great delight in what is truly rich."

As the CEO of your money, it's your responsibility to know where it is at all times. Think about all the money you've made or held in your hands throughout your lifetime. When you take inventory today, how much money have you kept? Set clear, measurable money goals.

OCTOBER 21

~~~~~~

My decisions are building generational wealth.

—Vivian Grafton

Proverbs 13:22

"A good man leaveth an inheritance to his children's children: and the wealth of the sinner is laid up for the just."

What are you doing now to leave an inheritance, not for your children but for your children's children? Do you realize that the decisions you make can have a lasting impact on your children's children? What decisions can you make today to affect the future of your children's children?

OCTOBER 22

~~~~~~

No matter the season, I will survive.

—Angela Thomas

Proverbs 4:7 (ESV)

"The beginning of wisdom is this: Get wisdom,
and whatever you get, get insight."

Who would have thought social distancing would be the
new norm? The world changed in the blink of an eye. These
are unprecedented times. Our loved ones can be here today
and gone tomorrow leaving us emotionally, physically,
economically, and psychologically impacted. Yes, it's a
paradigm shift, but God is still God. He wants us to lean on
Him, trust Him, and grow through this pandemic.
What strategies are you putting in place to survive?

OCTOBER 23

*My current circumstance does NOT dictate my future,
and I empower and employ thousands!*

—Anissa Green Dotson

Matthew 19:26 (NIV)

"Jesus looked at them and said, 'With man this is impossible, but with God all things are possible.'"

You have audacious dreams and goals inside of you.
A God-ordained dream will scare you. If you could accomplish it in your own might, it would not be of God.
Get on your knees, get focused, and when
He brings it to pass, give back!

OCTOBER 24

I remain positive and give praise to God
until I reach my breakthrough.
—Joyce Brown, 2019 Ms. Texas Senior America

Psalm 118:24

"This is the day which the Lord hath made;
we will rejoice and be glad in it."

Most days we face challenges that can result in a bad attitude. Do not give in to the negativity. Praise God despite your circumstances. Smile when you feel like crying. You are in control of your attitude. Only you can decide if you will have a good or bad day. When you smile and praise God, the negativity must flee. With a positive attitude, you will have the energy needed to accomplish your goals.

Soulful Affirmations

OCTOBER 25

~~~~~~

My tenacity pushes me through trials.

—Jenette Allen, EdS

James 1:2-3

"My brethren, count it all joy when ye fall into divers temptations; Knowing this, that the trying of your faith worketh patience."

Have you ever felt like you were in a battle? Tackling trials can be a tiring fight, especially if you feel the odds are against you. Do you know that you are the contender with Christ on your side? You will be deemed the champion! You will gain patience, peace, and perseverance because you were persistent. Have faith and stay tenacious throughout your trials to experience TRIUMPH!

OCTOBER 26

~~~~~~

I now have a sweet life, glorious peace, and an abundance of wealth.

—Lynder E. Scott, MBA

Romans 8:6 (ESV)

"For to set the mind on the flesh is death, but to
set the mind on the Spirit is life and peace."

Have you ever had stinking thinking thoughts such as:
"I wish I would have gotten my degree" or "I should be
married by now"? The list is endless. Right here, right now,
shut those thoughts down. Put on your adult underwear
and make it happen. God has stored greatness
inside of you. So, go be great.

Soulful Affirmations

OCTOBER 27

I will believe in the good of God's people.

—Meyett Lavalais

Romans 15:13 (NASB)

"Now may the God of hope fill you with all joy
and peace in believing, so that you will abound
in hope by the power of the Holy Spirit."

Never stop believing in the good of God's kingdom.
Do what is right even when others do wrong. God is aware
of it all and He will uplift those who are faithful to
His purpose. Continue to hold your head high,
check your inner circle, be mindful of what you are feeding
your spirit, stay faithful to His purpose, and He will
show up and bless. Just wait and see.

OCTOBER 28

I am intentionally praying in the Spirit, not with my intellect.

−Dr. Peggie Etheredge Johnson

Romans 8:26 (NIV)

"The Spirit helps us in our weakness. We do not
know what we ought to pray for, but the Spirit himself
intercedes for us through wordless groans."

Are you having one of those days when you desperately
need to pray? Are you overwhelmed with words that linger
within your heart but cannot escape your mouth? Holy
Spirit will verbalize your nonverbal expressions. Relax
and lean on Holy Spirit with every moan and groan. He
understands, intercedes, translates, and does the praying.

OCTOBER 29

I am healed and stronger every day.

—Shaundre Emmerson

Exodus 23:25 (NIV)

"Worship the Lord your God, and his blessing
will be on your food and water. I will take
away sickness from among you."

There were times when I couldn't get out of bed
and I was unable to speak to anyone because of
so much pain and sorrow.
Ever felt like you couldn't move, and your mind felt
paralyzed prohibiting you from doing anything?
Anxiety and depression had won the battle until you
realized your mind is so powerful it
controls how you feel physically and mentally.
Get up!
Stay strong, start moving, and choose to be
better every day. The healing begins when
you decide not to give up.

OCTOBER 30

~~~~~~

I will let my light shine bright.

—Shawntelle Y. Jones

1 John 1:5 (MSG)

"This, in essence, is the message we heard from
Christ and are passing on to you: God is light, pure
light; there's not a trace of darkness in him."

God is the true light of the world. As His children,
you have the same light in you. God wants your light to
shine bright even on your darkest days and through your
storms. It is not going to be easy, but you are
empowered to press through it all.

OCTOBER 31

~~~~~~

I will ALWAYS get up.

—Vivian Grafton

Psalm 37:23-24 (NKJV)

"The steps of a good man are ordered by the Lord . . .
Though he fall, he shall not be utterly cast down."

No dream, goal, or desire is without roadblocks or
opposition! Those are the times that we question the
dream, goal, or desire and if it can really happen.
Keep dreaming, pursuing your goal, and desiring to
see the end result. Even if you misstep or stumble,
GET UP and keep moving!

NOVEMBER 1

~~~~~~

I will give and serve with gratitude.

—Natasha M. Harris

Romans 12:11 (NIV)

"Never be lacking in zeal, but keep your spiritual fervor, serving the LORD."

It is an honor to give and serve because it allows us to shift our focus off of ourselves and onto others. What gifts do you have that can be used to serve? Serving is a form of worship and an expression of gratitude. What is your plan to start serving today?

NOVEMBER 2

I am established in faith; therefore, I speak gratitude daily.
—Bishop Richard S. Johnson

Colossians 2:7 (NKJV)

"Rooted and built up in Him and established in the faith, as you have been taught, abounding in it with thanksgiving."

Do you awaken each day with a grateful heart or a dreadful heart? When your faith is weak and your spirit is unappreciative, seeing God's blessings in a new day is arduous to impossible. When you become entrenched and established in your faith, your daily reflections will be consumed with God's abundance which is consistently accessible to you. Recalculate and honor God.

NOVEMBER 3

~~~~~~

Today is a gift from God.

—Juanita Payne

Ephesians 2:8 (NASB)

"For by grace you have been saved through faith;
and that not of yourselves, it is the gift of God."

What are you doing with the gift of today? Stop meditating
on yesterday and remember every good and perfect
gift comes from above. God gives us blessings without
expecting anything in return. What gift are you believing
God for? Make the most of every day.

NOVEMBER 4

I am happy, healthy, and full of life.

—Tammy L. Woodard

Philippians 4:4 (NIV)

"Rejoice in the Lord always. I will say it again: Rejoice!"

Happiness is a choice that we should make every day.
No one owns your happiness but you, so don't put it in
someone else's hands. Start each day with a spirit of
gratitude. Find your happy place and stay there. Make
your health a priority. Self-care is necessary for living
a fulfilling life. Live with no regrets.

NOVEMBER 5

~~~~~~

I will live my days as days of Heaven on Earth.

—LaToya Adams

Job 36:11 (NKJV)

"If they obey and serve Him, They shall spend their days in prosperity, And their years in pleasures."

Can you imagine how rich and satisfying life would be if we lived our lives according to the blueprint of obedience to Christ? Obedience to Christ is the hallmark of living a life where opportunity and favor is boundless. The sacrifice is worthy of the outcome. You will experience your days in life as days of Heaven on Earth.

Soulful Affirmations

NOVEMBER 6

I woke up this morning with clarity and strength.

—Marie Hart

2 Timothy 1:7 (NIV)

"For the Spirit God gave us does not make us timid,
but gives us power, love and self-discipline."

Imagine waking up one day and finding out that
everything that happened to you was all for a reason.
The ability to find simplicity in your life will empower you
to move forward with bringing peace into your world.
You may not understand all that happens but
understand that it happens for a reason.

NOVEMBER 7

~~~~~~

God hears and will answer all of my prayer requests.
—Melissa Powell-Harrell

Daniel 10:12 (NIV)

"Then he continued, 'Do not be afraid, Daniel. Since the first day that you set your mind to gain understanding and to humble yourself before your God, your words were heard, and I have come in response to them.'"

God hears and listens to us. He eagerly waits for our prayers so that He can answer them. He loves to hear our voices. Daniel was seeking clarity and understanding but soon realized that God was waiting to hear from him to give him the answer. We serve an awesome God that loves to hear from His children.

NOVEMBER 8

I know God will always have my back!

—Meyett Lavalais

Psalm 121:8 (AMP)

"The LORD will guard your going out and your coming in [everything that you do] From this time forth and forever."

God is protective over His kingdom, which means He is protective over you. There is no obstacle He will not see you through. You are never alone because you belong to Him. Remember that you are God's ordained assignment.

NOVEMBER 9

Everything I need is already available to me.

—Michelle Winfield Fuqua

2 Kings 4:7 (WEB)

"She went and told the man of God, and he
said, 'Go, sell the oil and pay your debts. You
and your sons can live on what is left.'"

What are you focused on? Sometimes, it is easy to get
distracted by what you do not have. Like the lady in this
story, you have a pot of oil which represents resources. Your
education, experience, gifts, talents, and ability coupled
with divine connections empower you for an abundant life.

NOVEMBER 10

I will no longer question what is happening to me; instead, I will know that everything is happening to help me grow.

—Necole Martinez

John 13:7 (NIV)

"Jesus replied, 'You do not realize now what I am doing, but later you will understand.'"

Have you ever asked God, "Why me?" Have you ever wondered why you are always the one going through hard times and experiencing break ups or unexplainable losses? God has a plan for our lives. Sometimes, He doesn't reveal it in the beginning. He needs us to trust Him blindly and He will bless us openly! We may not understand in the moment but in due time, His plan will be revealed and made clear!

NOVEMBER 11

~~~~~~

I will live each day with great joy!

—Renee Denise Fowler

James 1:2 (NLT)

"when troubles of any kind come your way,
consider it an opportunity for great joy."

We all have encountered trouble. No one is exempt. Yet,
when troubles and problems show up, the question we
each must answer is, "How should I respond? As believers,
when trouble arrives, we are to face it and consider it an
opportunity to express great joy! Things may not go as
planned, but we can choose to create great joy even amid
trials. Today, choose to express great joy in your life.

NOVEMBER 12

I will sow into the lives of others.

—Royleta Foster

2 Corinthians 9:6 (NKJV)

"But this I say: He who sows sparingly
will also reap sparingly, and he who sows
bountifully will also reap bountifully."

As Christians, it is our duty to help others. Sowing does not
always mean monetary giving. You can sow into the lives
of others with a simple phone call offering assistance with
tasks. How have you sown into the lives of others? See how
you can sow into the lives of others today.

NOVEMBER 13

God can use me to help someone else today. He will make me worthy.

—Ruby Jeanine Batiste

Ephesians 3:20 (NIV)

"Now to him who is able to do immeasurably more than all we ask or imagine, according to his power that is at work within us."

We've all experienced strong desires to help someone in need but may have felt unworthy of the task. The power of the Holy Spirit makes us worthy to be used by God to help others. Will you be obedient to the prompting of the Holy Spirit today?

Soulful Affirmations

NOVEMBER 14

~~~~~~

I will cherish every moment.

—Shameka D. Johnson

1 Thessalonians 5:18 (NIV)

"Give thanks in all circumstances; for this
is God's will for you in Christ Jesus."

Inevitably, time continues. It is impossible to go back in
time and make a bad memory good or vice versa. It is
imperative to savor the precious events that happen in our
lives, for they are all we have as we continue forward. Being
cognizant of not taking people or time for granted is a
sure way of cherishing each moment. Be grateful for every
minute. Think before you speak. Show love and kindness.
Make every moment a mindfully positive impression.

NOVEMBER 15

I awake with gratitude and choose to be happy.

−Dr. Sonya Wade Johnson

Psalm 90:14 (NIV)

"Satisfy us in the morning with your unfailing love,
that we may sing for joy and be glad all our days."

Have you ever had a song on your heart in the
morning that carried you through the day? Sometimes
that is God's way of refreshing our soul and encouraging
us to be grateful and happy in all things. We should always
seek to find happiness in our days so that we
can encourage ourselves and others.

NOVEMBER 16

I am worth it, worthy of it, and I am grateful.

—Anissa Green Dotson

Psalm 34:3 (NIV)

"Glorify the LORD with me; let us exalt his name together."

When was the last time you made yourself a priority? As we praise God for what He has done, it solidifies what He will do in the future. Accept God's goodness! Know that you are worthy of His blessings, and each morning give thanks and gratitude to our heavenly Father.

NOVEMBER 17

I will not apologize for being favored.

—Dr. Eric L. Holmes

Psalm 5:12

"For thou, LORD, wilt bless the righteous;
with favour wilt thou compass him as with a shield."

Lord, I thank You for blessing my life with Your favor. I will always celebrate You and never be ashamed to speak of how You blessed my life. Your favor has overwhelmed me and opened many doors. I love You and bless You, and never will I take it for granted the favor that rests upon my life. It was only You, God, that did it.

NOVEMBER 18

I am blessed beyond measure.

—Tara Johnson

2 Corinthians 9:8 (NIV)

"And God is able to bless you abundantly, so that in all things at all times, having all that you need, you will abound in every good work."

Sometimes we are so focused on what we are trying to achieve that we lose sight of what we already have. If we really take the time to think about all of God's blessings that He has already supplied, we would be reminded of how we already have enough. This act of thankfulness then prepares us to receive what God has in store for us. Every day is a day of blessings.

NOVEMBER 19

~~~~~~~~~~~~~~~~~~~~~~~~~~~~~~~~~~~~~~

I will count my blessings one by one.
To my fellow frontline workers.

—Sherry Wurgler

Psalm 28:7 (NLT)

"The LORD is my strength and shield. I trust him
with all my heart. He helps me, and my heart is filled
with joy. I burst out in songs of thanksgiving."

The COVID-19 discharge music resonated throughout the
hospital several times today.
Did it seem to come over the loud speaker a bit too loud?
No.
Let that music ring out crystal clear.
How joyous and heartwarming a sound that is!
Home to their loved ones they have missed so
much the past few weeks.
Home to the loving family embrace they missed
so much when they were sick.
Home to loved ones whose faces are not covered with
masks and paupers or bodies gowned from head to toe.
Frontline workers—you made that happen!

Soulful Affirmations

NOVEMBER 20

~~~~~~

I am grateful for my life's journey.

−Tara Johnson

James 1:17 (NIV)

"Every good and perfect gift is from above, coming down from the Father of the heavenly lights, who does not change like shifting shadows."

Everything that we are and have is a gift from God. Our life is a journey of lessons and blessings. Even when things do not go the way we planned, God is perfect in His timing. Let us celebrate and give praise for all that God has done in our lives. He is our constant and loving friend.

NOVEMBER 21

~~~~~~

I am worthy to receive all of God's blessings.

—Heidi Lewis

Proverbs 10:22

"The blessing of the LORD, it maketh rich,
and he addeth no sorrow with it."

Do you feel guilty or unworthy each time God blesses you?
Crossing every "t" and dotting every "i" isn't a prerequisite
for being blessed. These feelings may be causing your
heart to be filled with condemnation. God knows our
shortcomings. He says, "My grace is sufficient." In other
words, His grace has covered our shortcomings. God
desires to bless us. Lift up your head and with a grateful
heart receive every blessing He has for you.

Soulful Affirmations

NOVEMBER 22

I will work on being faithful to that which I am responsible for.

—Deborah A. Smith

Matthew 25:21 (NLT)

"The master was full of praise. 'Well done, my good and faithful servant. You have been faithful in handling this small amount, so now I will give you many more responsibilities. Let's celebrate together!'"

Faithfulness will take your relationships, your business, your prayer life, and your family to the next level. Being faithful over your responsibilities, whether great or small, is a set up for the bigger responsibilities that will lead to praise and celebration.

NOVEMBER 23

*I will continue to stay positive and prayerful
so that I can come out on top.*

—L. Lorraine Hale-Cooper

Psalm 34:4

"I sought the LORD, and he heard me, and
delivered me from all my fears."

In life, you don't know what will happen. But if you
pray and believe, you will rise above it all. You can ask
advice from seasoned elders and receive a "good word,"
but when you go hard after God, in due time you
will get what you need. Are you going to let God lead
and give you what He has for you?

NOVEMBER 24

~~~~~~

I believe that I can do anything.

—Dr. Sonya Wade Johnson

Job 42:2 (NIV)

"I know that you can do all things;
no purpose of yours can be thwarted."

There have been times when you felt defeated. God has
assured us, just as he did Job, that He can do anything.
The power He has given you is the assurance that all things
are possible, if you trust and believe. Keep trusting and
keep believing. Watch God work in ways that will manifest
blessings upon blessings for you!

NOVEMBER 25

I will swap pity for praise.

—Anitra Green

Romans 8:37

"Nay, in all these things we are more than
conquerors through him that loved us."

And the winner is . . . YOU! Weep, cry, and fret no more.
Swap the pity for praise and walk in the victory that the
Lord has promised you. Praise until you see a shift. Pray
until you see the change. Affirm the Word (of the Lord) until
you feel the Word strengthen you. You are more
than a conqueror . . . now, act like it!

NOVEMBER 26

~~~~~~~~~~~~~~~~~~~~~~~~~~~~~~~~~~~~

I am living my best life.

—Tiffany Mayfield

Psalm 37:4 (NIV)

"Take delight in the LORD, and he will
give you the desires of your heart."

What does "live your best life" look like? Living
your best life is exclusive to you. It is made up of the
people, places, and things that make you happy and it is
colored by what making a difference means to you.
God wants to give you the desires of your heart. Open your
heart and mind today and make it your best life.

NOVEMBER 27

I will sing in the rain and through the pain.

—Minister Kiesha L. Peterson

Psalm 59:17 (ESV)

"O my Strength, I will sing praises to you, for you, O God, are my fortress, the God who shows me steadfast love."

I have been through some storms and pain, but my God has made a way out through them all. It's not just about getting out, it's about going through. Sing praises to Him no matter what your situation looks, feels, or sounds like. You have the ability to praise your way through and out.

NOVEMBER 28

I will rejoice in every trial.
—Sonya M. Hall-Brown

James 1:2-3 (NASB)
"Consider it all joy, my brethren,
when you encounter various trials, knowing that
the testing of your faith produces endurance."

No one likes to face trials or trouble. You don't wake up
in the morning hoping for a bad day. However, we all
face troubles and trials. Right now, many of us are facing
difficult times. When you face a difficult time, trial, or
problem, God instructs you on how you should respond.
Are you rejoicing during your trails?

NOVEMBER 29

~~~~~~

No matter what comes my way today, I will speak positively.
—Dr. Sonya Wade Johnson

Matthew 15:11 (NIV)

"What goes into someone's mouth does not defile them, but what comes out of their mouth, that is what defiles them."

How many times have you allowed a situation to lead you to negative words? Think about how that situation could have been different if only you remained positive in your words. God encourages us to speak life to all things that we encounter. Speaking life brings about positivity that no negativity can destroy. Speak positively in all situations and watch God move!

NOVEMBER 30

~~~~~~

I am walking in God's alignment and I am in sync with His divine will.

—Marsha Taylor

1 John 5:14 (NASB)

"This is the confidence which we have before Him, that, if we ask anything according to His will, He hears us."

When was the last time you put your confidence and actions into the production of your creative thoughts and ideas? Did you know that your mind, your thoughts, and your actions combined produce your masterpiece in God's eyes? I challenge you to challenge yourself today! God is depending on you and the world is waiting for you!

DECEMBER 1

~~~~~~

I will have a victorious day, a victorious month, and a victorious year.

—Fatima Williams

1 John 4:4

"Ye are of God, little children, and have
overcome them: because greater is he that
is in you, than he that is in the world."

Do you rise out of bed in the morning commanding your
day? Do you see yourself victorious every hour, every day,
or every season? We have the greater one, our heavenly
Father, on the inside of us and because of this we are
walking champions. Know who you walk with and start
your day with confidence!

DECEMBER 2

I sow seeds that produce the fruit of the Spirit.

—Tammy L. Woodard

Galatians 5:22-23 (NIV)

"But the fruit of the Spirit is love, joy, peace,
forbearance, kindness, goodness, faithfulness, gentleness
and self-control. Against such things there is no law."

Have you ever been told, "You reap what you sow"
or "Treat others the way you want to be treated"?
In other words, if you do good, good will come to you.
If you do bad, in due time, bad things will happen to you.
But if you practice sowing the fruit of the Spirit,
you will produce a bountiful harvest!

DECEMBER 3

I will not mismanage my time.

—Dr. Eric L. Holmes

Psalm 90:12

"So teach us to number our days, that we
may apply our hearts unto wisdom."

We must cherish our days and never take them for granted.
Every day is a blessing from God and a privilege to see.
Allow wisdom and knowledge to help you on your life's
journey. Use the information you are given to learn
to make wise choices and decisions. Our days are
numbered and we do not know the day or the hour,
so enjoy and celebrate life while you can.

Soulful Affirmations

DECEMBER 4

I am a seven-figure entrepreneur.

—Tanya M. Turner

Proverbs 16:3 (NIV)

"Commit to the LORD whatever you do,
and he will establish your plans."

Are you spending quality time with God? In today's world,
as entrepreneurs we can get caught up in the trend of being
booked and busy. We can get so focused on making money
that we forget to include God in the plan. What are you
believing God for? Are you willing to commit
to God and affirm yourself?

DECEMBER 5

~~~~~~

I am dedicated to succeeding.

—Lashunda Denby

Psalm 20:4 (NIV)

"May he give you the desire of your heart
and make all your plans succeed."

What kind of success do you desire? There are different
kinds of success—personal, spiritual, social, and
financial—that you have to take into consideration in order
to achieve a balanced life. At times, we must ask ourselves:
Am I fulfilled? Do I appreciate life? Do I enjoy what I do?
These have nothing to do with tangible things such as
money, clothing, etc.

DECEMBER 6

~~~~~~

When I write it, speak it, and believe it, my vision will come to life.
—Yvette #theEXCHANGE McGill

Habakkuk 2:2 (NIV)

"Then the Lord replied: 'Write down the revelation and make it plain on tablets so that a herald may run with it.'"

I have countless testimonies of people I offered this Scripture to and they came back smiling and saying, "It worked. You said it." I quickly corrected them and said, "No, HE said it." If you do these three things, GOD will do the rest: Write the Scripture down, speak it out loud, and BELIEVE it with all of your heart. God's Word CANNOT return void.

DECEMBER 7

~~~~~~

God's timing for my life is a beautifully crafted masterpiece.

—LaToya Adams

Ecclesiastes 3:11a (NKJV)

"He has made everything beautiful in its time."

Sometimes life looks chaotic, bleak, and uncertain. Life's greatest lesson is that everything we could ever face— good, bad, or indifferent—works together for our good. The most beautiful masterpieces don't always begin that way nor do they look the same. Trust God's timing and commit to the process to become the beauty you desire to behold.

DECEMBER 8

I am one dream away from what I am meant to be.

—Marie Hart

Matthew 6:34 (NLT)

"So don't worry about tomorrow, for tomorrow will bring its own worries. Today's trouble is enough for today."

We cannot worry about tomorrow or run away from our past. Those things hold us back from fulfilling our dreams. Leave your worries at the door and step into the unknown to be the person that you want to be.

DECEMBER 9

~~~~~~

I am fierce and focused.

—Lashunda Denby

Colossians 3:2 (NIV)

"Set your minds on things above, not on earthly things."

We must strive for things above; we must strive for
better ideas and thoughts. One of the ways to develop your
focus is to establish daily, weekly, monthly, and yearly plans.
Set them in your mind then write them down on paper (or
in your electronic device). Where do you want to be next
year, five, ten, or twenty years from now? Make a daily to-do
list, even for minor things. That will help you to master
your mission(s). When you are unable to complete
a task, review and revise your plans.

Soulful Affirmations

DECEMBER 10

I will make better eating choices for my body.
—Dr. Madge L. Barnes

1 Corinthians 6:19 (NIV)

"Do you not know that your bodies are temples of the Holy Spirit, who is in you, whom you have received from God? You are not your own."

Watching how, when, and what we eat is important in the natural realm, but also in the spiritual realm. Poor eating habits can lead to diseases which could affect our ability to function optimally. Making better choices honors God who resides in our temple. What steps can you take today to optimize your eating habits? You can do it.

DECEMBER 11

~~~~~~

I rest well knowing my aspirations are assured by God.

—Jenette Allen, EdS

Hebrews 11:1

"Now faith is the substance of things hoped
for, the evidence of things not seen."

When lawyers plead a case, they submit evidence to the
judge and jury. That evidence can prove someone innocent
or guilty. What evidence has God given you to believe in
failure? Think deeply. On the contrary, He has given you
more evidence to believe in success! Use that evidence to
propel yourself into something great! Remember that you
will not always see a vision of success, but you have God's
assurance that it is coming!

DECEMBER 12

I will press to encourage myself every day. Courage will be my name.
—Michelle Franklin

Joshua 1:9 (NIV)

"Have I not commanded you? Be strong and courageous. Do not be afraid: do not be discouraged, for the Lord your God will be with you wherever you go."

Life has a way of challenging our belief that God's presence isn't with us wherever we go. He never tells us to do anything without giving us the strength and courage to do it. Overcoming fear of our own failures is key. When we submit, we run into courage.

DECEMBER 13

~~~~~~

I am a gift.

—Nina Gaddie Howard

Romans 12:6 (NIV)

"We have different gifts, according to
the grace given to each of us."

We have all been given specific gifts. Are you using your
gifts or burying them? All gifts, big or small, contribute to
God's plan. Write down your gifts and post them where
you can see them every morning. Then, focus on God's
blessings as He uses you for His amazing purpose.

DECEMBER 14

~~~~~~

I have everything I need to live Godly in Christ.

—Bishop Richard S. Johnson

2 Peter 1:3 (NKJV)

"As His divine power has given to us all things that pertain to life and godliness, through the knowledge of Him who called us by glory and virtue."

Have the current events manipulated you to believe you lack what is necessary to live Godly and virtuously? You may be surrounded by negative thoughts and insufficient human support, but God is divine; His omnipotent authority is sufficient to supply your needs before you ask. You will survive every temptation designed to keep you from living triumphantly in Christ.

DECEMBER 15

I accept prosperity into my life.

—Roni Benjamin

Proverbs 3:9-10 (NWT)

"Honor Jehovah with your valuable things,
With the firstfruits of all your produce;
Then your storehouses will be completely filled,
And your vats will overflow with new wine."

Can you relate to feeling unworthy of
a prosperous life? At the core of my excuses was the
fear of success. I challenge you to look over your
life and acknowledge your accomplishments so far.
Remember that you are wonderfully made and
dare to live up to your fullest potential.

Soulful Affirmations

DECEMBER 16

I handle conflict resolution with grace and ease.

—Tangie Barkley Robinson

Romans 14:19 (ESV)

"So then let us pursue what makes for
peace and for mutual upbuilding."

How well do you relate to others? We all have different
personalities, motivations, strengths, and hot buttons
that trigger us under pressure and can divide or unite us.
We must be more self-aware of how we communicate to
resolve conflict. We must learn to respond more effectively
by controlling our personality with prayer, affirmations, self-
development, coaching, etc. What personal development
course of action will you take to resolve conflict?

DECEMBER 17

~~~~~~

I have everything that I need inside of me.

—Royleta Foster

2 Peter 1:3 (CSB)

"His divine power has given us everything required
for life and godliness, through the knowledge of Him
who called us by His own glory and goodness."

Have you thought about going back to school or
starting a business but felt like you did not have with it
takes to do it? If God has given you an idea, you already
have the skills needed to be successful in class or in
running a prosperous business. Go ahead, write
your business plan or take a course.

DECEMBER 18

~~~~~~

I have sweet dreams.

—Melissa Shiver Sumpter

Proverbs 3:24 (NIV)

"When you lie down, you will not be afraid;
when you lie down, your sleep will be sweet."

Are there times when you can't sleep because you are
afraid of the unknown? The what if's? Well, stop worrying!
Go to sleep and rest in Jesus! Oh, how sweet it is to lie
down with no worries and sleep in peace. Sweet dreams!

DECEMBER 19

~~~~~~

I will live today as if there is no tomorrow!

—Renee Denise Fowler

James 4:14 (AMP)

"Yet you do not know [the least thing] about
what may happen in your life tomorrow."

We've all heard the saying, "Tomorrow is not promised."
Imagine if we lived each day giving life everything we
have—limitlessly giving of ourselves to God, our purpose,
family, and more. Living each day ALL IN! At the end of
each day saying, "I've spent today well. If it's the Lord's
will, I will give more tomorrow." What more could you
accomplish if you gave today your all?

DECEMBER 20

~~~~~~

I will get up, dress up, and stand firm.

—Nina Gaddie Howard

Ephesians 6:10-11 (NIV)

"Finally, be strong in the Lord and in his mighty power.
Put on the full armor of God, so that you can take
your stand against the devil's schemes."

How do you start your day? Even in the midst of uncertain
times, you must prepare yourself to rise up and press on.
When you rise, begin your day with prayer or meditation.
Then, confidently adorn yourself in your full amour and
stand firm. You can't help but to shine!

DECEMBER 21

~~~~~~

My life is being designed for the kingdom.

—Myoshi Robinson Thomas

Isaiah 65:17 (NIV)

"Behold, I am creating new heavens and a new earth."

My desire is to make sure that the kingdom is taken care of. I want my life to always be a reflection of the kingdom and a beacon of light for the world that creates new ideas, things, and places that will connect to the universe for the kingdom. When things are put out into the universe, the universe must respond.

DECEMBER 22

~~~~~~

I serve millions of people around the world.

—Shameka Oliver

Proverbs 19:17

"He that hath pity upon the poor lendeth unto the Lord; and that which he hath given will he pay him again."

As a vessel of the Lord, I will give to and help others who are less fortunate. And as long as I give selflessly, God will continue to bless me.

DECEMBER 23

~~~~~~

My family creates generational wealth.

—Shawntelle Y. Jones

Proverbs 13:22

"A good man leaveth an inheritance to his children's children: and the wealth of the sinner is laid up for the just."

Are you prepared to leave an inheritance for your grandchildren? Do you have a living will or trust? Most people do not like talking about having to transition once they die. This is usually because they are not prepared. You can prepare in advance for how you want your funeral, burial, assets, and estate to be handled once you pass away. This will help the next generation to advance.

DECEMBER 24

~~~~~~

I will live and not die and declare the works of the Lord.

—Alesha Brown, The Joy Guru

Psalm 118:17

"I shall not die, but live, and declare the works of the Lord."

God said this Scripture to me when I prayed for courage
and strength as a child to end my life. Today, regardless of
the circumstance or report, I speak LIFE. Know that no
matter what you face, you WILL NOT DIE, but you shall
LIVE and DECLARE the works of the Lord!

DECEMBER 25

~~~~~~

I have overflowing joy.

—Sonya M. Hall-Brown

Psalm 16:11 (CSB)

"You reveal the path of life to me; in your presence is abundant joy; at your right hand are eternal pleasures."

Joy comes from being in the presence of God. The closer you are to His presence, the greater your joy. I believe Jesus was a joyful person. I don't believe He went around with a pious frown on His face. To hang with Jesus had to be fun. Do you have overflowing joy?

DECEMBER 26

~~~~~~

I've already won!

—Shaundre Emmerson

Proverbs 3:5 (NIV)

"Trust in the LORD with all your heart and
lean not on your own understanding."

Have you ever prayed for something then tried to fix it
on your own? Let's have faith. We can't say we give it
to God then try to figure it out on our own. Patience is
hard sometimes, but it's so necessary. Seek God and His
understanding, for His way is the only right way out.
This was never your battle.

DECEMBER 27

~~~~~~

I am bigger than my Goliath.

—Minister Kiesha L. Peterson

1 Samuel 17:4

"And there went out a champion out of the
camp of the Philistines, named Goliath, of Gath,
whose height was six cubits and a span."

"Bigger is better." So they say. What do we gain by gaining
the world and losing our soul? We allow our problems, our
Goliath's, to make us lose focus of all that God has done for
us, is doing for us, and will do for us. No matter how small
or how big life's problems may seem, always remember
that God is bigger than them all.

Soulful Affirmations

DECEMBER 28

~~~~~~

I will soar to new heights.

—Juanita Payne

Isaiah 40:31

"But they that wait upon the LORD shall renew
their strength; they shall mount up with wings
as eagles; they shall run, and not be weary;
and they shall walk, and not faint."

Do you know that God wants to give us new strength every
day? Waiting takes patience and endurance. What are you
waiting on the Lord for today? Patiently waiting will have
its perfect work in us. Learn to wait because on the
other side you will receive the blessing.

DECEMBER 29

~~~~~~

I will change the trajectory of my life.

—Danette M. Brown

Ezekiel 34:26 (NLT)

"I will bless my people and their homes around my holy hill. And in the proper season I will send the showers they need. There will be showers of blessing."

I have often heard people say, "Position yourself and in the right season, God will bless you and open doors you cannot fathom." When you put your trust in God and believe, that becomes a true statement. What's hindering you from positioning yourself to receive God's blessings for your life? His love alone will pour down showers of blessings.

DECEMBER 30

~~~~~~~~~~~~~~~~~~~~~~~~~~~~~~~~~~~~~~~

I can make a fresh start today.

—Alicia L. Hemphill

Genesis 12:3 (BSB)

"'These men who were hired last worked only one hour.'"

Have you ever thought, "I don't have many years
left to fulfill my life's calling"? God's perspective
can span lifetimes. He rejoices when you look beyond
yourself to attach generational leaders to your vision.
It is never too late to accomplish something.
Who can you inspire with a fresh vision?

DECEMBER 31

~~~~~~

I take my rightful place.

—Traci Henderson Smith

Genesis 1:26;28 (MSG)

"'Let us make human beings in our image, make them
reflecting our nature . . . God created human beings;
he created them godlike, Reflecting God's nature.
He created them male and female. God blessed them:
"Prosper! Reproduce! Fill Earth! Take charge!"

Nothing is holding you back but you. You have the authority;
it has been vested in you. Take your rightful place!

Sources

Cheryl Polote-Williamson is a global media executive whose purpose is to help people share their stories and attain healing. She is the visionary behind thirteen bestselling books, including *Words from the Spirit for the Spirit*, *Affirmed*, and the Soul Talk series. She holds a Bachelor of Science in Criminal Justice and is also a certified life coach and the Executive Director of the 501(c)(3), Soul Reborn.

Cheryl has amassed numerous accolades, such as featured author at the NAACP and Congressional Black Caucus Conference, 2017 winner of the IALA Literary Trailblazer of the Year award, and Executive Producer of the Year for the stage play *Soul Purpose*. In addition, Cheryl's first film production was selected for the Greater Cleveland Urban Film Festival and the BronzeLens Film Festival. Her upcoming projects include *Soulful Prayers, Vol. 2* and the films *Saving Clarissa* and *Illegal Rose*.

Cheryl resides in Texas with her husband, Russell Williamson Sr. They have three children and two grandchildren.

Learn more at www.cherylpwilliamson.com

CREATING DISTINCTIVE BOOKS
WITH INTENTIONAL RESULTS

We're a collaborative group of creative masterminds with a mission to produce high-quality books to position you for monumental success in the marketplace.

Our professional team of writers, editors, designers, and marketing strategists work closely together to ensure that every detail of your book is a clear representation of the message in your writing.

Want to know more?
Write to us at info@publishyourgift.com
or call (888) 949-6228

Discover great books, exclusive offers, and more at
www.PublishYourGift.com

Connect with us on social media

@publishyourgift